A LOVE STORY FOR CLEVELAND

BY RON WATT

Kevin,
This is absolutely
good people
of a great
town! -
Best,
Ron Watt

12/3/01

©2001 Airport Books LLC

ISBN: 1-929774-11-7

Library of Congress Catalog Card Number: 2001093552

Layout by Francine Smith

Edited by Michelle E. Wotowiec

Cover Photo by Michael Hutchins

Submit all requests for reprinting to:
Greenleaf Book Group LLC
660 Elmwood Point, Aurora, OH 44202

Published in the United States by
Greenleaf Book Group LLC, Cleveland, Ohio.

www.greenleafbookgroup.com
www.airportbooks.com

Table of Contents

1 ISN'T IT ROMANTIC? • 1

2 JOE AND KATIE • 5

3 TERMS OF ENLIGHTENMENT • 13

4 ROCKY AND HERB TAKE A HIKE • 17

5 MORE TALKING BASEBALL • 27

6 THE CASE OF THE MISSING USHER • 35

7 BLUE RONDO A LA TURK • 41

8 BILLY THE KID RIDES AGAIN • 51

9 THE LAST ATTEMPT TO SAVE
THE THEATRICAL • 61

10 MEET MR. HENRY GERSPACHER • 65

11 THE MENTOR, THE MASTER • 73

12 DARK EYES • 81

13 FUNNY PEOPLE • 93

14 MORE FUNNY PEOPLE • 105

15 EVEN MORE FUNNY PEOPLE • 115

16 GOOD PEOPLE, DOING
GOOD THINGS • 121

17 STILL THE BEST SPORT • 131

18 WHY CLEVELAND IS COOL • 139

19 A VIEW FROM FIFTY-TWO • 149

20 SOME CASES IN POINT • 157

21 A GOOD GUY NAMED SAM • 163

22 REFLECTIONS OF YOUR
OWN LIVES • 167

23 WHY NOT FALL IN LOVE AGAIN? • 173

THE PEOPLE IN THIS BOOK ARE ALL REAL.
I WISH THEY ALL WERE STILL HERE.

THIS ONE IS FOR YOU, HANK.
"IN A MINUTE."

CHAPTER
ONE

Isn't it Romantic?

I have to admit, I'm in love with Cleveland for more reasons than one. This is a town that gets more than its fair share of raps. But I see it from a different mind's eye, always have and always will.

First off, I love the ethnicity and religious persuasions. Unlike Boston or New York, for example, there aren't weightings here of two or three ethnicities. We've got them in droves, Germans, Irish, Czechs, Slovenes, Latinos, Italians, Lebanese, African-Americans, Syrians, French, Hungarians, Lithuanians, Jewish-Americans, Poles, Estonians, Romanians, Islamics. If I didn't mention your ethnicity or religion, please forgive, for there are more than 80 ethnic groups and every religion known to man in the Cleveland area. But you get the idea. And you know something? In Cleveland these ethnic groups are known to blend together and their kids are an exotic mix of hues and profiles. That is why, for example, so many beautiful women are here, and so many have become models because of their distinctive, worldly "looks."

I grew up in a neighborhood called Collinwood, the part near Euclid Beach. My mother is Slovene, and my dad was half Scottish and half Swiss. Twenty-nine years after my 1943 entrance into the world I married a woman who is half Lebanese and half Syrian. I guess you could call our kids Americans! I can tell you this: they don't look like native Californians.

This is my story of my Cleveland, and maybe it will make you recall yours. This is a story about yesterday and today. It is a story I've been waiting to tell, but I had to pack in 57 years of experience to be able to tell it.

My first recollection of anything was around 1946, when my uncles came back from military service. I remember meeting them at the Terminal Tower that then seemed busier than Hopkins Airport seems today. Somehow I see this picture in black and white, just like the photos you remember from Times Square, when the soldiers and sailors came back home at the end of the War.

Then it was a bit of blur until the later 1940s when I headed on to kindergarten at a grand old school, Memorial Elementary on East 152nd, right next to where the Lakeview school burned in the tragedy of 1908 that killed 172 children and two teachers. On the site where Lakeview stood was a pool and garden in memory of one of the worst disasters of the 20th century. At that pool, in my youthful years, I had great fun trying to grab the plumpish frogs that proliferated there. Of course, my mother and grandmother told me not to do it, "'cause it will cause warts on your hand, Ronnie." I wasn't sure I believed them because the older boys at Memorial would catch them all the time, and they didn't seem to have warts on their hands.

I grew up in two places in the 1940s and early 1950s, Trafalgar and Huntmere Avenues, both close together in Collinwood. My Slovenian grandparents had a home at 15700 Trafalgar; along with that home came a big chicken coup, and two gardens, one in front and one in the back. The back garden was actually like a little farm, with every crop imaginable. Now that space is asphalt, the parking lot of Key Bank. In the front, were plum and apple trees and in the house was love.

Each spring, I could watch baby chickens hatching from eggs in an incubator that was on the closed-in back porch. I can still smell the downy fur-feathers of those little chicks. They smelled like a fragrance powder. And it was always fun when a rooster was one of the little chicks. The rooster was always dark, instead of the yellow fur ball baby hens. I watched these chicks rapidly grow and move on to the hen house, where they laid eggs for the family. Eventually they ended up in a stew. And, yes, I have seen chickens with their heads cut off, and, yes, they ran around for several minutes until my grandfather could catch them and he would pour their blood in a pail and feed it to the dog, who acted like this was some kind of delicacy.

My grandparents had an old collie dog who couldn't stand noise and one summer during the Fourth of July celebration at nearby Euclid Beach he had enough and croaked. His name was Arrow. He had been with me my entire boyhood. It was traumatic, so my grandparents immediately obtained another dog, this one a beagle. Unfortunately, it turned out that he had distemper and one day when I was eight and delivering the neighborhood newspaper and walking Mickey, he had a fatal attack. I tried carrying him back home, as he jolted and spasmed and frothed at the mouth, but it was no use. I put him down and watched him die on a neighbor's tree lawn in Collinwood.

You know something, though? Most of my days growing up in the old neighborhood are remembered with good thoughts. It was fun growing up in Cleveland in the late forties and through the fifties. The War was over, Truman, then Ike, was in the White House, and accept for that other War, in Korea, things were pretty damned fine. People were, more and more, becoming upwardly mobile. So were we and so we moved to Euclid in 1952, but I spent plenty of time at my grandparents on Trafalgar.

⊢⊣◆⟶○⟵◆⊢⊣

CHAPTER
TWO

Joe and Katie

Somehow, Joe and Katie, my grandparents, met in Ely, Minnesota. Somehow they found each other in that ore-mining town along the Mesabi iron ore range. They both came from villages in what is today the country of Slovenia. Joe Champa was born in 1888 and Katie Tomc in 1892. Joe came from Nova Mesta, near Italy, and Katie from Metlika, right on the border of Croatia.

When they met, he was an ore miner, and she worked in a boarding house in Ely, which is so far north you have to bundle up in August. They met in the boom days of America following the turn of the last century. Between 1915 and 1922, they had four children, two girls and two boys. My mother, Molly, was the second child. For some reason, Joe got sick and tired of the mining and coldness and he got the bug in his head to return to the old country. That they did in the twenties, the boys going to live with him on a farm he bought and the girls staying with Katie in Ljubljana. Why the family split up I never quite understood. But for the most part they were separated for a time back in Slovenia. Then around the time of the Great Depression, Joe decided America was the place to be - again. He had a friend, Streets, who was working at Fisher Body in Cleveland and Joe thought this would be a good place to work and live. Katie later got a job as a cleaning woman at Collinwood High School. Neither of them drove a car, although they had a car. Nonetheless my grandfather rode a bike or took a bus wherever he wanted to go.

They raised their crops and chickens right there at 15700 Trafalgar, and they taught me some good things too.

They always tried to speak English when I was around. In some ways I wish they had spoken more Slovenian. To this day I remember quite a few of the words but I really can't speak it, though my mom, aunt and uncles certainly did, because of their side trip to the old country.

What Joe and Katie taught me was the foundation to my whole life. They exposed me to music - good music - and they pushed me, especially, to read books. I think for several years I won the summer reading bee at the Memorial Library for consuming the most books and giving reports on those books. They had a glider swing on the front porch and I would recline on the swing all summer and absorb books about General Washington, President Jefferson, Benjamin Franklin and books about geography.

When my parents would go out on Saturday night, so did my grandparents and the latter would take me with them. We often went to the Croatian Home on Waterloo Road, a place that houses today, in part, the Beachland Ballroom, home to every kind of eclectic live music from all over the country that you can think of. So when I was little, about four or five, they would take me to the Croatian Home and I would hear great tambaritzan bands. I enjoyed them so much that I would refuse to leave until they put their mandolins and guitars back in the cases at 2:30 a.m. The same was true if we went to the Slovenian Home down the street on Waterloo. I wouldn't leave until the band guys quit.

So, naturally, they got me a 12-base accordion, and I started to play. Then, later, in 1951, they got me a 120-base accordion that I still have today. Joe and Katie paid close to $2000 for the unit, a Petromelli from Italy, back then.

What can you say when your whole life was music growing up? If I could have rewritten the script I wouldn't. It was nice growing up at 15700 Trafalgar and 16402 Huntmere playing music and walking up and down either street and hearing more of the same. At one house there was a bassist, another a drummer, then a sax player, another accordionist, a banjo player, a guitarist. Wasn't hard to find a jam session. I've always wondered if a kid growing up in Gates Mills or Hunting Valley could ever have experienced anything like this.

When you grew up in the same neighborhood that Frank Yankovic or Johnny Vadnal or Johnny Pecon or Georgie Cook or Eddie Habat and Kenny Bass came from you were in paradise in those days. These all were national recording artists on RCA, Mercury, Decca and other big time labels in those days. And I got to hear them in person. Sometimes from their front porches.

I remember when I really took to the accordion, I'd play all the top hits - "Just Because," "The Blue Skirt Waltz," "The Too Fat Polka," "The Tic Tock Polka," "The Socialaire's Polka," The Iron Range Polka" - most of which were huge million-selling records. We'd go down to Florida in the late forties, and they'd be playing all of Yankovic's stuff on the glass-bottom boats. Yank was all over the place and the other guys weren't far behind in fame. And this was all happening out of my neighborhood in Collinwood!

One of my favorite things was going to the old Log Cabin at Euclid Beach for the Addressograph-Multigraph (where my mom worked) family picnic and listening to Johnny Vadnal. I loved his band, which included his two brothers, Tony and Frank. Tony and Frank did a lot of singing as they played. Tony was a great bass player who earlier was an accomplished violin player who had to stop that after he lost a couple of fingers in an accident. Frank was superb on the guitar and banjo. And Johnny, well, he held it all together on the accordion.

Many years later, I started studying the music of Johann Strauss Jr. and then I realized how close the Slovenian-American music was to the Viennese. If you don't feel good listening to this, you aren't alive. In my teens I cultivated an interest in jazz, realizing that the Slovenian-American music I was playing was similar, in that it was improvisational. Funny, how do you compute Count Basie with Frank Yankovic. Somehow I did and I loved them both, mainly because they loved their music and their audiences and, of course, the audiences everywhere loved them back.

Yankovic's band was so popular that in a couple of national "battle of the bands" they beat out Duke Ellington in the finals. The Duke said he's never going up against a polka band again.

Any of the above musicians, especially the worldly Ellington and Basie, swung to their own beat. I was wondering the other day what these bands would have sounded like if they were run by huge corporations instead of cool cats who slept, ate and drank music. That was the way of Yank, too, traipsing about the country and overseas, too.

When I was a kid Yankovic was so famous, he and his band did several Hollywood movie shorts that trailed main features at theaters across America.

• • •

Just down the street from my grandparents on Trafalgar was a pie factory. It smelled like pies - cherry, apple, blueberry. I still think of the penetrating, sweet aroma to this day, even though the pie factory is long gone.

Every day - and I mean every day - I'd go down to the pie factory for my grandmother and with the 25 cents she gave me I'd buy a half dozen glazed donuts that were startlingly fresh. I'd watch the women there pull the donuts right out of the hot oil and then out of the glazing pot and - voila - there'd be the fresh donuts. I'd do this at lunchtime from elementary school. Always I would eat one donut on the way back to my grandmother's. And sometimes another two at her kitchen table. Lots of energy obtained for the rigors of school in the afternoon. I could have turned into a tub, eating them and the Vienna bread my grandmother made from scratch. When I was even younger, a favorite trick was scooping out the bread from under the crust, leaving a tunnel with a closed end. This was the one thing I would do that would send my grandmother yelping in Slovenian. I didn't know at the time whether she was swearing or just yelping. I couldn't resist myself, I was sort of addicted to this procedure. The one word I do remember her uttering is pronounced phonetically - dee-vee-yawk - which translates into "devil" in English.

But, what the hey, this was a part of growing up that today I treasure.

The other transgression I recall - and this occurred only once and I don't know what possessed me to do it - was when I was making some mud pies in the backyard of her home and decided to come into the kitchen and throw several of them on the ceiling. I've never heard of anyone else ever doing this since. It must have been a warning sign that I was going to go into the creative business at adulthood. Or it could just be that I was a borderline asshole who was seeking attention, which I still do today.

I remember another time when my grandmother stoutly came to my defense when a neighbor, an old German lady, told her across the backyard fence that I had called the lady "a dirty name." Grandma Champa told me the old lady said I called her "a big fat skunk." My grandmother asked me why I did that. I said I did that because the lady had called me a "Pollack." My grandmother called the old lady back and said she shouldn't be calling me names like that and she deserved what I had said to her. Love.

And I remember another time when I was about eight and very sick with the flu after school, a time when my grandfather would give me two nickels and I'd go down to the corner store for a bottle of Pepsi and some potato chips and return home to watch Pinky Lee on TV. This day I was too sick to move, and my grandfather noticed it. He put his big, huge hands around my little ones and made them warm. Kids don't realize sometimes that these hands that seemed so big were probably just normal size. But when you are small everything seems big. He made me feel better, safer even though I was sicker than a dog and lethargic. He was my grandfather.

Many years later, when he and I were standing in front of Katie's casket, he, a man of few, short, concise words - a man of undeniable humor as well - looked up at me and said, "Grandma, shot, no good, don't work no more." This he said about the woman he and I both loved and adored. This the love of his life, the mother of his four children. It must have torn his heart out to lose her. His quaint way of expressing his feelings that day I will remember for time immemorial.

My grandfather himself was to die exactly one year later, in 1972. He was 83. Nobody should feel sorry for him. He had a good, long, happy life.

When he died, my recollection of him was from some years earlier when he and my grandmother were thrown a 50th anniversary celebration. We had taken over the party room of a long-since gone Euclid restaurant. My grandfather celebrated like only he could do, so much so that my two uncles thought it was time for him to be taken home. My grandfather didn't want to go, and as they tried to carry him off horizontally into the night he grabbed the doorframe of the party room and he wouldn't let go. This was quite a sight. They'd pry one hand off the frame and then try the other but by then the first hand was back on the frame. This went on for some 10 minutes. He was determined. Finally, he gave up and gave a big wave to everyone in the room. That was my grandfather.

When he died, I also remembered the time he helped my father Archie lay floor tile in the new rec room my father had impeccably built over the course of a year. The result was an absolutely perfect first half of the floor. They decided to take a lunch and beverage break at the chagrin of my Uncle Bernie, who was helping them. He wanted to get the job done and get on to other things and "not screw around" as my Slovenian grandfather and Scottish-Swiss father were wont to do at most any occasion. The second half of the tile - the portion set in the afternoon tile-laying session - was all cockeyed and off course and had lots of black glue oozing from the seams. It was a lasting testimony of two guys from two terribly different backgrounds and generations having a good time. People had fun for years laughing at their work whenever a party was held in the rec room on Halle Drive in Euclid.

CHAPTER
THREE

Terms of Enlightenment

My first job ever was when I was about eight. I used to stack cans at Kuhar's Grocery Store on East 156th Street, near Trafalgar. I had known Mr. Kuhar since my early days in the neighborhood and he thought I'd be perfect at stacking cans.

One time when I was about six, my Uncle Bernie, the youngest of Joe and Katie's kids, who was in his mid-twenties at the time, had a grand idea. He had the impression that I fibbed a lot. Made up stuff. Which was true, of course. That's why I write books.

He thought it would be a dirty little trick to send me on an errand. "Ronnie," he said, "you should go down to Mr. Kuhar's and see if you can get a liar's license." So I dutifully went down the street to Kuhar's and asked the guy if I could buy a liar's license for the quarter my Uncle Bernie had given me. I think Mr. Kuhar said he was out of them but he'd have some in soon, so I should come back. Mr. Kuhar and my uncle had a lot of long-time laughs over that one. It is enlightening when you are just six years old and you find out you've been duped. At least I was an earnest liar who had every intention of getting that license.

Down the street from Kuhar's was a tavern, at the corner of 156th and Waterloo. Basically, there was a tavern just about anywhere you looked around the neighborhood. On that particular corner always stood some young adult men, hanging out smoking cigarettes and telling stories. One of those guys was Danny Greene, who had yet to become the well-known mobster. I used to deliver The Scoop weekly newspaper on Thursdays. I liked that corner because usually around five p.m. when I was making the deliveries those guys would treat me to a candy bar. Usually an Almond Joy. If Danny were there, you could bet money that I'd get that special gift. Years later at the Theatrical Grill, which I'll talk about later, he was exactly the same, buying me drinks.

But back in the old neighborhood, everybody always seemed to be having a good time. I still can see those young guys smoking cigarettes and drinking from long-neck P.O.C. beer bottles. When I was a kid I looked up to them and wished I were their age so I could be part of the gang.

Speaking of beer, I learned the fine art of sitting at a bar from my grandfather Joe. Often, he'd come home from Fisher Body, pick me up at the house and take me to the Croatian Home on Waterloo. He'd have about six fishbowls and a couple of shots and I'd have my usual, a Pepsi and some chips. I liked sitting with the older men who had come from their jobs in ritual to discuss the day's events. There was something sturdy and traditional about this all and it made me feel kind of like a man. And I was next to my grandfather whom I worshipped. He stood about five-eight and was strong as an ox. He had a ruddy complexion, a full head of brown hair, darting blue eyes, and arms and a chest that had never seen a weightlifting gym but looked like they did.

I've never seen anyone scale a ladder or scamper about on a high roof like he could. He was a good carpenter, plumber, you name it. He made good wine, good blood sausage and prepared a fine wild rabbit. He thought it was good to leave the buckshot in the rabbit, even though you could break a tooth. He thought it tasted better with the buckshot in the meat.

He was unique but I'm sure people of my generation who grew up in neighborhoods that had high numbers of immigrants can tell similar stories about these colorful people. Maybe you have some of your own. Somehow when I hear about athletes talking about courage on the playing field or even business people talking about the courage it took to start a company and keep it going, I am not sure this sort of courage has any measurement to the courage those people from Europe, the Middle East and elsewhere had when they rode steerage across an ocean, with little money in their pockets, sometimes no friends or connections and land somewhere and try to make it. Somehow I think they and their predecessors made America, more so than a guy whizzing down a football field staunching off a stampede of opponents who are trying to smash him into the ground. The glory the immigrants had was in producing their sons and daughters and grandchildren, most of whom have gone far beyond the successes of the people whose unstinting fortitude enabled this all to happen. And many of the immigrants fought for this country as hard as they would have fought for their homelands in the great wars of the 20th century, even the 19th century.

It is good for the soul to remember what they did.

CHAPTER
FOUR

Rocky and Herb Take a Hike

My first job was stacking cans at Kuhar's grocery store, my second was delivering *The Scoop*, the old Collinwood weekly paper, and my third was rather spectacular as far as I was concerned. It happened at the beginning of the baseball season in 1960, the year after the Indians made a good run for the pennant against the Chicago White Sox. The Indians had a good team in 1959, with Tito Francona hitting .363 and big name guys like outfielders Minnie Minoso and Jimmy Piersall.

Most famous of all, though, was Rocky Colavito, the matinee idol in right field. A guy who could throw a perfect strike to third base from the farthest reaches of Municipal Stadium. He also was a big homerun hitter who is one of few players ever to hit four homeruns in one game. That he did in Baltimore in 1959, landing himself on the cover of national news and sports magazines. As I recall, he almost had five in a row because the next game he sent a ball deep to the leftfield fence and it just missed being a homerun. Most Indians fans would probably agree that no player was ever adored more than The Rock. And another guy that was not far behind was Herb Score, one of the most talented lefties in baseball history. People thought he was the next Lefty Grove but a bad thing happened to Score in May of 1957 when Gil McDougald of the New York Yankees hammered a ball to Score's right eye. Herb was never the same afterward.

The Indians traded Score to the White Sox before the 1960 season and Rocky went to the Detroit Tigers for batting champion Harvey Kuenn. That trade really rocked me and the rest of Cleveland. General Manager Frank Lane, "Trader" Lane, or "Traitor" Lane, did the unimaginable. He traded The Rock. People went nuts, and by the way, the Indians went to hell in 1960 in spite of an exciting 1959 team. This seemed to send the team and its fans into a funk the recuperation from which took until essentially the mid 1990s.

My third job was to be a member of the Indians grounds crew and later one of the helpers in the home team and visiting team clubhouses. I was 16 at the beginning of the season in 1960. I was elated at the opportunity to have this job because I loved two things then: baseball players and sportswriters. I wanted to be a sportswriter. I figured I'd learn a lot with this. But as much as I was hunky dory with this great job for me, I was crestfallen that the great kid from The Bronx, Rocky Colavito, wouldn't be there in the dugout with me.

It was a rough and cold first day on the job. My friend, Bob Ross, and I proudly wore our groundskeepers uniforms. Blue tops with the Chief Wahoo insignia on the left side. White pants and white shoes. Even though the temperature was around 40 degrees, maybe 38, that early April, we wore no jackets or other paraphernalia because we wanted everyone to know we were special. We were on the grounds crew headed by the famous groundskeeper of his time, Emil Bossard.

Many of the kids on the grounds crew came from St. Joe's High School. I was one of only a few from Euclid High.

That first year several things happened to me that were life forming. That year and the next year I saw so much baseball, at least 160-some games, crappy baseball, that my love for the game soured. I didn't go to a game for a good 10 years after that experience.

Ironically, the lackluster Indians propelled me in another direction, the direction of the street, Short Vincent to be specific and it was there I found an incredible array of characters, Toulouse Lautrec-like characters, bounding around in a weird carnival of extremes.

While the Indians were playing ball I would sneak out for a few innings and walk up East Ninth Street to Short Vincent. There were two reasons for that. One was the bookies, the hoi polloi bar and restaurant crowd, the dancing girls (some of whom were doing more than hoofing), the politicians, the police, the swirl of humanity that all seemed to me to get along and have a damned good time. The other was my aural nerves were attracted to the music I was hearing from the loud speakers on the marquees of the clubs. The jazz.

I'm sure the Short Vincent scene wasn't as monumental a jazz street as in the earlier hey days of East 105th Street and up and down Cedar where dozens of clubs existed, but for me, in my time, it was splendid. At 16 and 17 I was way too young to get into the clubs on Short Vincent, Ninth Street or Chester Avenue, but I did enjoy strolling by them. Mostly, I'd do this by myself. I was drawn to this area like a moth to a flame and what I heard and, somewhat saw, gave me a new course in music appreciation.

I'd like to sit on the curb in front of The Theatrical Grill, which was the most hoppin', joint on Vincent. The gents who played that club were a pantheon of the straight-ahead, bop, post bop and modern jazz stars. Joe Venutti, the great, swinging violinist; tenor sax greats Coleman Hawkins and Ben Webster; Oscar Peterson, the next best thing to Art Tatum on the piano; trumpeters Muggsy Spanier, Roy Eldridge and Jonah Jones; pianist Marian McPartland and her cornetist husband Jimmy; trombonist Jack Teagarden; Bill "Honky Tonk" Doggett on the Hammond B-3 organ; pianist Dorothy Donegan; drummer Cozy Cole; and singer-pianist Glen Covington were just some of the musicians who played there. Others who played there earlier, like Dave Brubeck, Stan Getz, George Shearing and Tony Bennett had gotten so popular that they performed mostly in concert halls by the time I was sitting on the curb on Short Vincent. But if they were touring through Cleveland, they would often stop in as patrons. So did the likes of Woody Herman, Count Basie, Stan Kenton and even Duke Ellington. Movie and TV stars too. George Raft, Milton Berle, Danny Thomas, Bob Hope, Jane Russell are some who come to mind.

I probably had the opportunity to hear just about every top jazz group in the world those two years, even though I couldn't see them, unless they stepped outside for a cigarette or two. People would line up in twos down the street to get through the red rope of the Theatrical. I always knew it as the Theatrical Grill, but after a catastrophic fire that destroyed the original Theatrical, Mushy Wexler, the owner, changed its name to the Theatrical Restaurant, perhaps thinking that this would be an upgrade from just a grill. But I like the sound of Theatrical Grill better.

. . .

Back on the ball field a lot of interesting things were happening, even if the team was a bore to me without Colavito. That is not to say the players were bores. Oh no, not Jimmy Piersall or Gary Bell or Mudcat Grant. I especially liked Vic Power, the agile first base man who once stole home twice in a game during my time with the Indians. Power was so good, he could play any position and occasionally did, so the club could spark up the entertainment level for the fans. The catcher was Johnny Romano, who joined the Indians from the World Series winning White Sox along with third baseman Bubba Phillips and pitcher Barry Latman.

Latman astonished me with his ability to chew tobacco and gum at the same time. Yes, watching him put all that stuff in his mouth was gross. We also had a young backup first baseman, Walter Bond, who could juggle three baseballs with one hand. He was a potential superstar but was struck down not long after with leukemia.

Piersall, who was an incredibly gifted center fielder also was incredibly crazy. But I always liked the guy because of the grit with which he played. He liked to bait the umpires too. One game at Yankee Stadium he went and sat down behind the three monuments that used to be at the back of the outfield and he refused to come out because of being upset with a call.

Piersall had a brood of at least eight kids and he would let them come to the ballpark and run all over the place, while he played baseball with the grounds crew and clubhouse guys out in right field. Emil Bossard, the head groundskeeper, wouldn't let us play on the main diamond because we would have destroyed it. When you are 16 and 17 playing out in right field with real major league ball players is just fine. Others who would come out were Bob Hale, who was the hottest pinch hitter in the game at the time. He played more with us than he got to play for the Indians. The second baseman Johnny Temple, whom we obtained from the fine Cincinnati Reds team, was hurt for a while and couldn't play second. But he did throw me a lot of knuckleballs, which he liked to practice on the sidelines. I played a lot of catch with Bubba Phillips, too.

Also, the manager, Mel McGaha, and his coaches used to ask some of us kids to pitch when players wanted extra batting practice. Sometimes we'd throw an hour at a stretch. I'd work on my sliders and curves and it would piss off some of the players to no end when they whiffed four or five times. Mike del a Hoz, a young infielder, I swear, couldn't hit my curve ball. He'd feast on my fast ball. Sometimes I'd throw him the knuckler Johnny Temple taught me. He couldn't hit that either. You can guess he didn't have much of a career.

When we weren't on the field we'd like to sit upstairs in left field near General Manager Frank Lane. This is how I learned to say every swear word in the book. That's all Lane did. Always deeply tanned and in his sixties by this time, Lane was a notorious trader of players. He's the guy who got rid of Colavito, Minoso, Score and some of the other more colorful players.

One night George Strickland, a pretty good fielder at third, jumped away from a line drive down the line and Lane had a fit. I won't say what he said here because I'd like this book to be of some use to families. Nonetheless, he went on a tirade for the next couple of innings. That night was the last we saw of old George Strickland for a long time.

I mentioned that boredom would set in with the play on the field, so we, my friends and I on the crew, would invent things to occupy our time. One gambit that we enjoyed was going up on the roof of Municipal Stadium, way up on top, high above Cleveland and the baseball field itself, and dangle our legs over the ledge, right above home plate. It usually took about an inning for the umpires to notice this and then they would hold up the game. The players, Mudcat, Gary Bell, Piersall and Vic Power, especially, would encourage us to do this, because, of course, in the end, they were bored with everything too.

My favorite recollections of what happened when boredom set in were these:

In the men's johns there were tall garbage and rubbish cans that contained all kinds of contaminants, including mustard, peanut shells, melted candy apples, partially eaten hot dogs, spit, puke, you name it and we would take great delight in getting two of the grounds crew guys to heave ho the contents of the cans over the top of a stall while some guy inside was doing "number two." We were fast in those days and even if we weren't we could still get away from a guy with his pants down taking a crap.

The best dumping we ever did involved custard cream. This one I invented with my friend Bob Ross, who is now a priest in Cincinnati. We were standing in the upper deck looking out a window when we spotted a fire chief polishing his red car below. It was nice and clean and shiny and he was putting the finishing touches on the hood.

Bob and I would eat the custard from large paper cups. Usually we ate two or three of those a game, among all the other junk, like peanuts, hot dogs, Pepsis, chips and hot pretzels.

Sometimes you just can't eat any more custard, so, instead, we looked out the window and turned one full cup upside down. The first custard rolled downward in something that looked like a short, thick white rope. It landed on the fire chief's hood in what appeared to be a small white circle, which he suddenly noticed, probably thinking some rotten-ass pigeon had hit the car, just after he had spent an hour cleaning it. Well, that wasn't all. Another white ball hit the hood a few seconds later. Now the whole front end of the car and part of the fire chief had turned sticky white, and we were on our way, never to be caught but laughing uncontrollably for the rest of the boring game.

• • •

A side note to all this is that while I was with the Indians, we had something very interesting happen in 1961. Two guys, Mantle and Maris, were trying to shag the home run title that Babe Ruth had owned since 1929. They were trying to knock off 61 homeruns to set aside the Babe's big year of 60 homeruns, and like the Babe, they were with the Yankees.

A few years earlier, when I was just hanging out at Municipal Stadium for autographs, I remember Roger Maris riding out of the park in the back of a car with Larry Doby, the first black player in the American League and a true combine of power, batting average and fielding. Doby was the old-timer and Maris was purely a rookie with the fulfillment of promise ahead of him. Later, Maris was to be traded to the Kansas City Athletics and, as was the custom, he would end up with the Yankees because, though the Athletics were a major league team, they were in reality a farm team for the Yankees. He joined Mantle, one of the most gifted ever to play the game, and together they produced one of the best power combinations in history

Their stories have been depicted many times, so I won't go much into that. But I was there to witness the grind that became the 1961 power drill to break Ruth's record. During my time with the Indians, these guys would show up in Cleveland several times a year and they would usually beat us. But the story of the two M & M guys became a national, if not international, story because they were on the same team and they were each trying to best Ruth's long-standing record.

I remember Mantle as fun loving and pretty friendly. Maris, like Oklahoman Mantle, grew up away from the bright lights. Roger was from Hibbing, Minnesota, also home of Bob Dylan. But the Mick had been around New York City for a long time. He knew Toots Shore's and all the other haunts and he knew how to handle media pressure.

Roger Maris, on the other hand, found the pressure too much to consume. His hair began falling out, he became curt and inward. But the good news is he chased Ruth's record through 162 games and beat the Bambino in the end with 61 home runs, albeit with an asterisk because the Bambino had accomplished his feat in the 154 regulation games of 1929.

I can say I was there, on the visitor's bench, when the M&M boys went after each other for Ruth's title. Sitting there with us — and of course I was just a fly on the wall — was a little bespectacled man with white hair, Red Smith, from New York, perhaps the best sports essayist of his time. He was a quiet, thoughtful and pleasant man.

I got just as many osmosis vibrations from him as I did from the M&M boys.

More about Red Smith and the other great writers I met as we continue …

CHAPTER
FIVE

More Talking Baseball

They didn't come any better than Red Smith. His writing was so spare and clear you couldn't edit him. He bounced around the various New York City newspapers of his time, always finding another job when the current paper he was working for would go out of business. During his career-span, there were at least eight New York dailies and he had been with more than several of them. You can read Red Smith today and he still sounds good and is timeless. I still enjoy reading his special compendium of columns in book form, *To Lost Friends*, which chronicles much of his best production on the newspapers for which he worked.

But let me say, Cleveland had its own share of good writers back in my time growing up. They were Whitey Lewis and Frank Gibbons and Bob August of The Cleveland Press, Gordon Cobbledick and Jimmy Doyle of The Plain Dealer, and Hal Lebovitz and Ed Bang of The Cleveland News. Later, Lebovitz would move over to a long career as sports editor and columnist of The Plain Dealer after The News folded. There were others, like Regis McCauley of The Press and Ed McCauley of The Plain Dealer, who entertained me as a youngster trying to read all three of Cleveland's newspapers.

Reading Bob August was a lot like reading Red Smith. A penetrating essayist, Bob cranked out 700 words five days a week at The Press. All good writing, nothing bad. He still writes for the Lake County News Herald to this day. Anybody wanting to get into or understand writing should read his stuff.

When I was with the Indians in '60 and '61 there were plenty of broadcasters to meet as well. The big time national guys were Mel Allen, Lindsey Nelson, Curt Gowdy, Dizzy Dean and Pee Wee Reese. For the Tribe we had Jimmy Dudley and Bob Neal and Harry Jones, a former PD writer who became a broadcaster. Moreover, we had Ken Coleman, who did both the Indians and Browns games, and was one of the best broadcasters in America. Bill McCulgen was another who worked with Coleman on Indians and Browns telecasts. And there was one other, an older guy, who had a great career earlier and sometimes filled in for these guys. His name was Tom Manning. One Yankees-Indians series in Cleveland, where there were 80,000 people in the house each day or night, Manning, the old-timer, filled in on radio for Bob Neal, who had suffered a heart attack, and I can't remember when anyone was better on the air. Another thing, the Indians, unbelievably, won all four games against the Yankees in that series with Manning at the helm. One of the few highlights during the Indians demise.

The Browns were clearly a better team. When you were on the grounds and clubhouse crews in those days you usually had the opportunity to work for both the Indians, and Browns games. The Browns were clearly a better team, with Paul Brown still at the helm. Jim Brown and Bobby Mitchell were the two best running backs I have ever seen in a backfield. Brown was the power, slicing guy, Mitchell the guy who would run right in the face of an opponent, throw a head fake and zoom in another direction. We traded away the rights to Mitchell for, like Brown, another Syracuse star, Ernie Davis, whose career as a pro never got off the ground, for he, like Walter Bond, contracted leukemia. The thought was that that would have been an even better backfield than Brown and Mitchell. The quarterbacks were largely lackluster. One was Milt Plum, a fine player at Penn State, whose greatest claim to fame in the pros was that he sold to the Indians the giant neon rotating Chief Wahoo sign that hung above the southeast gate of Municipal Stadium. Plum worked for a local sign company in the off-season. The other quarterback was Jim Ninowski, who threw the football so hard that nobody could catch it.

The grounds and clubhouse crew had a lot of fun when the Indians would play a night game on Friday, a day game on Saturday and a twi-night football double-header Saturday night. Then on Sunday morning we'd switch the field back to baseball. No sleep and you made about six dollars for each game, baseball or football. If you were crafty you'd find a way to catch two hours of "zzz's" on the trainer's table in the home team clubhouse each night. Somehow all this got done and everything looked good on national television.

When I remember Jim Brown from those days, seeing him close up, I remember a guy who was fast and strong as hell, had the physique of Adonis, with a 32-inch waist and a weight of 232 pounds. Few guys found it easy to bring him down and I think that if he were playing today he'd still be a marvel and maybe hold all the records. Remember, he played in 12-game regular seasons, while the guys today play 16 games.

. . .

And one last baseball story. This is the first and last time I got close to Rocky Colavito. Too close. Flash forward to the mid 1970s. Rocky is now a coach for the Kansas City Royals. He is about 46 years old and my wife and I meet him at the old Blue Fox Restaurant at West 117th Street and Clifton Boulevard. The meeting is not intended.

The Blue Fox had been closed for a number of months for remodeling. My wife Simona and I enjoyed the Blue Fox for a number of reasons before it had been remodeled. The food and drinks were good. They had a good piano player, Jan Paderewski. It was a classic hangout and a great place to people watch.

When we returned with great anticipation after the remodeling, to our dismay we found not the dark, clubby Blue Fox but instead something that looked like a disco.

The maitre de gave us "one of the best tables in the house." This was a table, among others, that had been set up on a sort of shallow stage surrounded by a curtain of eight-foot high beads, glistening from lights of variable hues shining on it from various angles. It was the complete opposite of the way the Blue Fox looked before, and it was uncomfortable.

Simona asked if I could get us another table. I knew the maitre de would not be happy about this after he thought he gave us one of the best tables in the house. I requested a change, and he obliged with a clear note of obstinacy.

Next, we found ourselves at a two-top in the back right next to the kitchen door. This would now be as good as it gets.

Shortly after we ordered our drinks, a tall, grey-haired gentleman walked in and was seated at the next table, with his back to the wall, next to my wife. Immediately a sextet of other patrons, on the other side of this gentleman started bugging him. Meanwhile, I held up the menu so the gentleman could not see my gesture, and I pointed toward him, whispering, like a Bob Newhart-routine, to my wife that "look carefully, that's Rocky Colavito." On the other side of him a guy is saying, "Hey, Rock, meet my mother-in- law, meet my wife, my brother-in-law; let me buy you a drink, it's good to see you, Rock."

Colavito, who doesn't drink, didn't want a drink and he didn't want to be bothered, just some good food and he'd be on his way. My simple mission was not to bother the Rock in the least way. It was good enough to be sitting next to my hero.

The drinks they made at the Blue Fox were big. My wife's hand is small. She had a big Manhattan on the rocks. As I looked at her, and she snuck a peak at Colavito, I noticed something horrifying. It was her drink slipping from her small hand, ever so slowly as if in time lapse. There was nothing I could do, the damage was happening and happening before my eyes. We had a disaster and we were going to make a fine mess of Rocky Colavito.

The freeze frame stopped and The Rock was now brushing the cascades of Manhattan juice from his snappy light pink sport jacket. He was covered with the stuff and I was devastated. I looked directly into the eyes of Simona as if I were an executioner, then to Colavito. First I said I'd get his coat cleaned. I'd buy him a new coat. My intention was not to bother him at all, I said. In my mind this was a sorrowful moment, the Great Colavito, who doesn't drink, now smelling like he was a candidate for the City Mission.

He was irritated but quickly said, "This is not the first time that's happened." I kept apologizing and glowering. But soon it was just an accident, and the man I didn't want to bother started talking and talking. He ordered us some special soup from the chef, ordered our dinners and went on talking about everything on his mind, especially after I asked him if he could be a designated hitter, even at age 46, and he said yes he could and he said the rotten stupid asses in baseball would have nothing of it however. Rocky was always confident, especially about his batting. He was never in a slump. There were times he went 0 for twenty or worse but he was never in a slump.

· · ·

OK, I've got one more about Colavito and one quick one about Mel McGaha. First Colavito.

I said I had never met him until the tragic Manhattan-spilling incident at the Blue Fox. Well that isn't exactly the case. In 1957, when I first really started going to Indians games, Rocky had come up again from the Indianapolis farm team, where he had been a phenom. Yet, not too many people were very familiar with him in Cleveland at the time. I remember standing outside the stadium waiting for autographs. He wore a light tan jacket and was handsome with jet black, curly hair. Almost no one asked for his autograph, though I did because it was easier to obtain than that of one of the more familiar players.

But the next year, 1958, Rocky had risen in such stature that the kids would come by the hundreds to get his signature. It got to the point where they were mobbing him. His solution was to sign every request but he said he wanted them to be courteous and stand in single file. They did and the line went around the entire circumference of the stadium.

The other story is about 1962 Manager Mel McGaha. He had replaced Jimmy Dykes who had replaced Joe Gordon. In fact Trader Lane had actually traded managers in 1960, sending Gordon to Detroit for Dykes. Both of these guys were famous from their star-filled playing days.

But the next year we had a coach who was a new manager in waiting. He had never played a game in the Major Leagues but he was Lane's choice for the next iteration of the Indians in 1962. He seemed like a nice guy, much younger than Dykes.

I used to do special favors for the players and coaches and the manager. One job was signing baseballs for them, so they wouldn't have to bother themselves with this chore. By my doing this I allowed the guys to spend more time playing cards, smoking cigars and telling stories in the clubhouse.

For half a season I signed coach Mel McGaha's name to balls. And one day I was sitting next to him with a whole box of balls that I was signing, and he looked down and said, "Kid, I can't thank you enough for signing the balls for me, but I wish the 'F' you would spell my name correctly."

CHAPTER
SIX

The Case of the Missing Usher

The stories from the lackluster 1960 and 1961 Cleveland Indians are bountiful, both on and off the field. One of the most impressive to me was that of an 18-year-old Sam McDowell warming up on the sidelines in demo mode just after he had signed with the Tribe. The lefthander was so fast that smoke seemed to come out of Bill Lobe's catcher's glove. Lobe was the bullpen practice catcher. McDowell was throwing along the sidelines near the Indians' dugout.

Danny Kravitz, a catcher for the Kansas City Athletics, was watching and just kept shaking his head. He said to a teammate, "There ain't no way I am ever hitting against that guy and I would never catch him," as one fast ball after the other popped Lobe's mitt. The more Sudden Sam threw, the more players from the Indians and Athletics came out of their clubhouses to watch.

Everybody thought this was the fastest pitcher they ever saw. And he probably was.

Sam went on to lead the American League in strikeouts a number of seasons and he should have been headed to the Hall of Fame, except that he had trouble with the John Barleycorn. Not the night before he pitched but all the other nights. Stories about Sam hitting the Cleveland bars are legend. He was a good-time Charley. Many years later he recovered from these endeavors and today is a successful consultant to professional sports teams on issues of substance abuse. He and many fans wonder what could have been.

. . .

Not all the stories about the colorful people from back then involved players. One night against the Yankees on national TV we had an hellacious rainstorm. It was off and on for a while but even in the night skies you could tell something really ominous was going to happen. We had pulled the tarp on the field and taken it off a couple of times in the early innings. By now we were already soaked to the bone.

Sometimes not enough kids showed up on the grounds crew and the Bossards, the family that ran the crew for years, had to improvise. This they did by importing ushers from the stands. Some of these guys were in their forties and fifties, out-of-shape and slow. Some of them weren't that busy because often there were a lot of empty seats back then and they were available for other duties. They would put on coveralls and come down to the grounds crew box in left field to be of help, if called. Often they were of no help, because the kids, ranging from 16 to 20 were much quicker and stronger.

When you put the big tarp on the field more than once, removing it and rolling it back up, it would become heavier and heavier, from the weight of water and caked-on dirt. Then on top of that, with a heavy rain falling as you took the tarp back out, it became close to unbearable to pull.

Sometimes we'd have to run the tarpaulin out to the outfield to get some of the water off, and then run like hell back to the infield and hope with the wind and a good non-stop trot we could sail it back to the infield. Then we'd run like hell right into the Indians dugout for cover. A few crewmen would stay out briefly to stake the tarp down if it were windy.

For the players, this seemed to be their greatest joy. It always was worth a lot of laughs because invariably someone would fall down during the journey and come in looking like a mud-laden version of the Michelin man. When the kids fell down, they were usually quick enough to get up and regain the tarp. Sometimes for the pinch-hitting crewmembers, the ushers, it didn't work that way.

On this particular night with the rain coming down in torrents on our third run for the medal, we unrolled the tarp, ran it out to past second base, took it back into the outfield to dump the water, flipped it to the other side, and ran the sheet toward first base and "home." There was one little problem; next to the left of me was one of the older ushers. I could hear him huffing and puffing early on and it sounded like he was going to have a heart attack. I wondered if he was going to make it. He didn't.

Around the area of the pitcher's mound where the guy had to run up a pretty steep hill, he stumbled and went down head first, but we kept right on going. Now the guy was inside the tarp, all this being watched by millions on national TV, with Mel Allen at the mike. Everybody in the stands, at home, in the beer hall and even some of us, notably me, knew what had occurred. In the rush to get to the dugout I don't know what I was thinking but when I sat down on the bench I had just about forgotten - or didn't want to believe - what had just happened seconds earlier.

The guys staking down the tarp were finishing their jobs and then making their run for the dugout. The players were laughing and laughing and applauding, for this was a far better show than what they could possibly have provided. And much faster paced.

Meanwhile, there was a sort of bubble moving around beneath the tarp right around the pitcher's mound. I was so soaked and had so much rain in my eyes that I was having trouble focusing. Then I started to panic. Technically, I could have been blamed for this tragedy. I could have tried to grab him, I thought. But then, I thought, we both would have gone down. I felt sorry for the guy and I figured he was probably going to die under there. His moving around underneath the green tarpaulin had people, I'm sure, everywhere busting a gut. Some of the players near me were folded over in laughter and in tears. Vic Power was shaking and rolling on his back on the dugout floor and Piersall's beady eyes were swirling like pinwheels.

Of course, this guy had to be rescued. And it was a tough job because there was so much water on the tarp. The crewmen went back out and had the damnedest time even getting it a foot off the ground. A bunch of the players came out to help, and that was the only way we'd have enough manpower to rescue the poor slob. We finally pealed the tarp back to the pitcher's mound, and there was the guy lying on his back seemingly breathing his last breath, totally covered with mud and chunks of grass. We dragged him back to the dugout, to a standing ovation, then up the alley to the clubhouse and to a waiting ambulance. He didn't die, but he must have come damned close. He never tried to help us again.

. . .

One of my other favorite things to do when I was bored was to go out to the visitor's bullpen and sit out there with the pitchers and catchers. Some of the jokes I didn't understand but they always made me and one or two of my friends on the crew feel like one of the guys when we'd be out there.

I remember a very young Jim Katt, a left-hander with the Washington Senators before they became the Minnesota Twins, bugging me for Good & Plenties and Bazooka bubble gum. He couldn't have been more than 19 or 20, just a couple of years older than me. He didn't get to pitch much back then but most everyone following baseball knows he went on to become an outstanding southpaw who lasted a good couple of decades in the bigs and since has had a fine second career as a broadcaster.

Sometimes the visiting players bugged me for things a little more elaborate than candy. For example, a well-known catcher asked me if I saw a blonde sitting in the lower leftfield seats, right by the large portal between the stands and the bleachers. I said I did. She was a robust blonde of about 30, with thick makeup.

The catcher asked me if I would approach her with his hotel room number. This was not easy because I still had trouble with shyness with women of this nature. But I welled up all the grit inside of me and gave her the note. The catcher gave her a wink and a wave, and the next day he gave me 25 cents for my good deed. I think he must have had a good time that night.

Funny thing, I began to notice that woman at most of the games, no matter the team in town. She always sat in the same spot, one deck below the great Frank Lane, the general manager, who could not see what was going on but probably would have found it more fun than watching his ball team through his binoculars. I don't know whether I was a messenger boy or a pimp but there were many requests for her company. Her name was Marilyn and, looking back, she may have been more famous through the league than some of the players.

CHAPTER
SEVEN

Blue Rondo a La Turk

Before I was even a teenager it was the practice of our family to go to the Art Museum for Easter. My mother Molly got me all decked out in a suit and tie, and for some reason I got her to buy me a pork-pie hat. Probably so I could look like my father and the other gentlemen milling around the reflecting pool. I recall my father wore a homburg. I think I chose a pork-pie because I thought it was hip, like the musicians wore.

Even back when I was 11 or 12 it made me feel good to get all dressed up, especially so on the great fashion day of the year - Easter.

Moreover, there was something mystical that drew me to University Circle each year and today as a middle-aged adult I am still drawn to it, more so than ever. To me, it is spellbinding and today the best it's ever been and during the next years will get even better. There is no place quite like it on earth. No place with so many cultural and educational institutions nestled so close together in such a magnificently beautiful setting. And it is so serene.

Everywhere you look today there is construction. Exciting new things happening in the Circle. At the Botanical Garden a massive undertaking will bring new buildings that will represent a "scoop" of Madagascar and a "scoop" of Costa Rica, one a desert and the other the opposite, a verdant jungle. Both will have indigenous flora and fauna, and will change what was once a nice garden center for blue hairs and blue blood into a national tourist attraction.

Not far away, new construction is taking place as well at the Museum of Natural History, which is installing a new telescope and other amenities. And at the Art Museum, a significant expansion will add more mass to house the museum's extensive permanent and touring exhibitions. A world-class architect will be hired soon.

At the Cleveland Institute of Music plans are under way for a new capital campaign that will refurbish the early 1960s building, add a larger distance learning studio, many more teaching rooms and a new concert hall. And around the corner, the Western Reserve Historical Society will expand its exhibitions once the Crawford portion moves downtown to become the Crawford Museum of Transportation and Industry.

Check out the architecture of the fairly recent Kent Smith Library down the street, the library for CWRU. They don't make buildings like that any more, people say. The Smith Library is an exception of gothic grandeur. Next door, on East Boulevard and Euclid Avenue, stands the magnificently refurbished Severance Hall. The main hall glistens inside and quite frankly makes Carnegie Hall seem only normal by comparison. The neo-classic, art deco stage encasement is much brighter than the old blondish orchestra shell. Passageways throughout the building have been greatly enhanced to permit case of access from the recently completed giant underground garage adjoining Severance. An elegant new restaurant has been added, and everything else has been spiffed up.

Not far away is the new Frank Gehry-designed Peter Lewis building at CWRU. This spectacularly shaped combination of exposed steel and brick will be home to the Weatherhead School of Management. And not far off University Circle, Cleveland's Health Museum will double in size and completely replace the present building. Each room will be interactive to patrons and school groups and each room will be a virtual TV studio, beaming up programs to classrooms across America.

And some people say not much is going on in Cleveland. Go to University Circle, I say. It will mesmerize you.

• • •

I think you have gotten the idea that I like music, from the earlier pages of the book. Yes, it has shaped my life and that of many others.

One thing that totally fascinates me about University Circle is the Cleveland Institute of Music, which draws the most gifted students from all around the world. When you walk into its doors you are instantly awash in all sorts of musical voices - strings, horns, reeds, piano/percussion/tympani and, of course,

the original instrument, the human voice. There is a gently set-
tling feeling just walking through the lobby hearing what might
seem like it should be discordant sound. But it isn't. You should
do it, too, and you can do it for free. Just walk into the lobby
during any semester, stand next to the guard desk and listen. If
you listen, it will amaze you. It has been said musicians are God's
angels and I believe this to be so. The spirituality of it all is pal-
pable, if you listen.

Recently, I had two unforgettable things happen to me
on back-to-back Saturdays. One took place in Kansas City and
the other at University Circle.

In Kansas City, in the famed Country Club Plaza area
(the oldest continuing outdoor shopping mall in America) I
heard a group called the Scamps, jazz musicians whose origins
date to 1946. The youngest guy is probably over 70 and some of
the others are in their 80s. They play that Kansas City jazz sound
that makes everyone smile. If you're not sure what that sound is
like, think Count Basie, who really was from Red Bank, New Jersey, but made it big with his band from Kansas City. Or think
Charlie Parker or Jay Mc Shann. The first number I heard them
play was "Shiny Stockings," a colossal Basie-written jazz chest-
nut. I had my nine-month-old grandson on my knee and I swear
to God we were both in paradise. We were at a club called Plaza
Three, which has operated for 36 consecutive years, quite a feat
in the jazz club business. We were there as a family. My daughter Laurie lives in Kansas City with her husband Mark. My wife
Simona and daughter Mandy, from Chicago, and son Ronnie,
from Cleveland, were all there with young Campbell Reece
Robinson. The parallel for me here is it reminded me of the
times many years ago that my grandparents would take me to
hear music. This particular little guy responds to the vibrations

and was completely absorbed by the sounds, never falling asleep and never getting finicky. The Scamps all play well, very well, all five of them. It was a night to be remembered.

The next Saturday back in Cleveland, I had the distinct pleasure of attending the Cleveland Institute of Music graduation. Now there aren't many graduation ceremonies that turn me on; usually they're too long and too boring, except of course when your kid crosses the threshold to receive his or her diploma.

The CIM graduation is nothing like this at all. It's a graduation you don't want to end. Wonderful music played by gifted young men and women who will be going off to see the world. Many will play for the greatest symphony orchestras in the land and overseas. That's how good CIM is, ranking right up with Julliard, the New England Conservatory of Music, the Curtis Institute and the Peabody. I have been a guest at two successive CIM graduations and I hope they keep asking me back.

The 2001 graduation was very special to me because one of my musical heroes was receiving an honorary doctorate. That would be Dave Brubeck, one of the most innovative jazz men of the past century and still playing handsomely at age 80.

Dave Brubeck should have been a cattle rancher. His dad ran a 40,000-acre cattle ranch in Concord, California, and that is what Dave, who is part American Indian, thought he was going to do. But that career took a side tour when his interest in music led him to begin playing in bands in his early teens, performing in San Francisco and environs. By the time he was in his 20s, he was a legitimate star on the rise. After time out for active military duty in the Second World War, Dave went back to the Coast and started developing contrapuntal rhythms in 5/4 and even more complex timings. This began to catch on and by the late 40s and early 50s the West Coast jazz sound that he was instrumental in spawning began to emerge as its own. Brubeck was becoming a prominent national and international figure.

One of his most famous albums of the time was "The Dave Brubeck Quartet at Oberlin." In the early 50s, he was on the same programs with Duke Ellington. One day, I think it was in 1954, Dave got a knock on his door. Standing there with a Cheshire grin was the Duke. Behind his back Ellington was holding something. Dave inquired as to what it was. Ellington produced a copy of *Time* magazine, and on its cover was Dave Brubeck. This was a nice gesture by Ellington, but the modestly quiet Mr. Brubeck was crestfallen. He didn't feel he deserved the honor. No, he thought, Duke Ellington should be on the cover.

Brubeck's reverence for Ellington was such that he wrote a tune in 1955 that is called the "The Duke," which many of you know as the theme song from the Charlie Brown animation shows.

Well this day in May in 2001 I got to witness something quite remarkable. On the musical program at the graduation was a piece called "Blue Rondo a la Turk," a big Brubeck hit, along with "Take Five," which were both on the seminal "Dave Brubeck at Carnegie Hall" album of the early 1960s.

Two of the graduating students played on opposite-facing nine- foot concert grands. And they played brilliantly. They took two or three bows, and then came back from the wings and leaned over to shake hands with Dave Brubeck, who was sitting in the front row. It was a snapshot in my head that I won't forget. One of the students was from Bulgaria, Georgi Slavchev, and the other from China, Karl Lo, and they had come together to honor

Dave Brubeck, who came originally from California and should have been a cattle rancher. And all this happened at Kulas Auditorium at the Cleveland Institute of Music in University Circle in Cleveland, Ohio. That's why I love my town.

I have another Brubeck story. This one took place a few years ago at the Power House in the Flats. Dave was supposed to perform on a big concert grand at Nautica Stage. As he and his wife Iola (she always travels with him wherever he goes) watched the Weather Channel from their hotel room, they became alarmed at the heightening electrical storm that seemed to be hovering right above downtown Cleveland. They called their manager, Russell Cloyd, to see if it would be safe to perform on the outdoor stage. It became clear the storm was probably not going to let up and it was decided to move the concert into the large banquet hall at the Power House, just across from Nautica Stage. This meant Brubeck would not be playing on a nine-foot concert grand as planned but instead a Baldwin upright console piano. Not a daunting problem to Dave at all, as he said, "I have these Baldwin consoles in different rooms in my house in Milford, Connecticut. I'll be right at home."

And so he was, starting off with the St. Louis Blues and taking his band right through the Brubeck repetoire and then some. The sound was not unlike that of a jazz club of yore, brick walls and all, some people seated in chairs, some standing and some seated on the floor. About 400 in all. He got more out of that little piano than most players could get out of a concert grand. He got his long-time side guys, Jack Six on bass, Bobby Militello on sax and flute, and Randy Jones on drums in a groove and they kept at it, a remarkable feat considering the last-minute change in venue. They played acoustically. There was virtually no amplification in the makeshift facilities. The audience went wild. Truly an improvisational experience not soon to be forgotten by the Cleveland crowd.

The next day, I took Dave and Iola Brubeck to the Music School Settlement, which was the beneficiary of the previous afternoon's fund-raiser concert. He was enthralled to watch a children's concert orchestra go through practice at the Settlement, another one of the gems of University Circle. Easily, he asked the kids questions about their instruments and about what they liked about music and their answers came easily in return. His eyes sparkled at the give and take. His quiet, gracious demeanor belies his ability to play a "big" piano with strength that today at age 80 is remarkable.

Next, he asked me to drive him by some apartments on the outer edges of University Circle, just west of 105th Street. He said that he and Iola and their four young children often stayed there for weeks at a time when he was playing in and around Cleveland. One of the places he played was the Theatrical Grill.

He said, "We used to play this room where the stage was right in the middle of a big bar. I'll never forget that. It was a jazz club of jazz clubs."

So I took him down to Short Vincent and into the Theatrical, which was still alive, barely. It had not yet turned into a stripper joint with a rough and tumble sports bar downstairs. We walked into the Threatrical and he remembered the harlequins on the walls and the big bar, which was not so big anymore because the owner had decided to cut it in half to allow for more dining tables and a bigger dance floor. The bandstand was now in back of the room, nowhere near as formidable as when the band sat above the 60 or 70 people crowded around the bar, with another 120 people seated at surrounding tables. I think Brubeck felt a nudge of nostalgia but was probably happy that most of his career past the early '60s found him in the most important concert halls in the world. 'Twas a day goneby that we witnessed that day and never would witness again, at least at the Theatrical.

CHAPTER
EIGHT

Billy the Kid Rides Again

When I think of the last of the hey days of the Theatrical I think of Billy Martin, the man who managed many teams in baseball and was always one of the best until he ultimately self-destructed. One of his favorite places in the U.S. was the Theatrical Restaurant and you would see him there often in the 1970s and into the 1980s when the place was still going pretty strong.

Billy had been coming to the Theatrical since the 1950s, in the old building known as The Theatrical Grill. He'd bring with him a young Mickey Mantle, the veteran outfielder Hank Bauer and a young pitcher named Whitey Ford during the salad days of the Yankees in the early 1950s. They and a few others formed their own "Rat Pack," and one of the haunts of this pack was the Theatrical, especially. And for decades he kept coming back.

Martin always found the "T" a home away from home. There he would have two or three scotches lined up on the bar, always a line of drinks. Often these would come from patrons who might have been just as colorful as Billy.

Now Billy wasn't just sitting there drinking mind you, he was working. Often he'd have a couple of young ball players and he would be giving them instruction. He'd stand up and swing an air bat a few times, showing his players a thing or two about batting. He'd crouch as if to receive a high bouncer in the infield, or he'd step back as if in the outfield, catch an air ball and then throw it to the cutoff man. He'd huddle with his lieges and look around the bar and wave thanks to a patron for sending him a drink.

If you'd ask him, he'd tell you about the one season he played for the Indians. That was 1959 and he was considered a great addition at second base, but an injury shortened that season for him to just 73 games. Still, he liked to talk about how the Indians finished just five games behind the White Sox for the American League pennant. He thought the Indians had a better hitting team, which they did with 167 homeruns to Chicago's meager 97 homeruns and with a league-leading team batting average of .263 and a slugging average of .408 vs. .250 and .364 for Chicago. Also, he said the pitching was better. The Indians led the league that year with 58 complete games to Chicago's 44, but the White Sox had the most saves, with 36, and that might have made the difference, he said.

The years I used to see Martin at the Theatrical were when he was either managing the Yankees, the Oakland A's or the Yankees again. His best effort was with the 1977 Yankees, who took the World Series, 4-2, against the Los Angeles Dodgers. He came in first five times with the different teams he managed. In addition to the Yanks, his other pennant winners were Oakland, Minnesota and Detroit. Only at Texas did he miss winning the American League pennant. This guy was wired and he added to the electricity in the air at the Theatrical.

He'd undoubtedly have continued coming into the "T" into its last days in the '90s. But he encountered a mishap one winter day in 1989 when a truck he was riding in took a nose dive off a hill near Johnson City, New York. That was the end of the pugnacious (he once got into a fight with a marshmallow salesman in Minnesota and lost and was involved in countless other fisticuffs on and off the field throughout his career) but always effervescent Billy Martin, and baseball is the lesser for it.

• • •

When I first started going into the Theatrical in the early 1970s, they still had a red rope to control the crowd. You had to have a reservation or get there early in the evening to get a seat, or you waited your turn at the door, sometimes into the street, like in the older days when things were really hopping.

Things started to slow through the 1970s, but it was still a lot of fun, with the most interesting personages imaginable populating the bar and the banquettes. Shondor Birns always took the first banquette on the left as you came in. You would have never known he was one of the major mob and racketeering figures in America by his demeanor, which, to me, was always pleasant and accommodating.   He knew everyone who was a regular at the Theatrical. They included cops, judges, insurance salesmen, brokers, PR and advertising guys, hookers and priests. In the Theatrical one would find a veritable family of people who would come in every afternoon or evening.

One of the guys that came in was Danny Greene, another noted mobster and foe of Shondor Birns. Although in earlier days they had been associates, I don't think I ever saw them talk, though they talked with everyone else. Danny was one of the guys that used to stand at East 156th and Waterloo, in front of one of the many bars in the neighborhood, and get me Almond Joys when I was delivering the weekly paper. Now he was buying me drinks, just because I was sitting near him at the Theatrical. Danny, of course, was the consummate character. He was tall and fairly slender and had red hair. He most always wore green, wrote in green ink and drove a green car. He was proud to be Irish.

Guys like Nino Rinicella, a bartender at the Theatrical for more than 50 years, would make sure everyone knew everyone else. And when I started coming into the "T" as an adult of 29, after a decade of living outside Cleveland, he introduced me to Danny. I knew who Danny was and I knew he had had major ties to the longshoremen's union and had later expanded his business horizons. What those were I was not exactly sure. Of course, we never talked about that kind of stuff, mostly sports and politics or about some good-looking "broad," as Danny would put it, across the bar. I don't ever recall Danny letting me buy him a drink.

I learned a lot at the bar. One of the older bartenders, Al, a slicked-back, gray-haired warrior, taught me how to make the "best Manhattan in the world. Trust me! You take Maker's Mark, the best bourbon in the world, but first you put in some sweet vermouth, preferably Stock vermouth, but not too much. Then you pour in the Maker's Mark, preferably a lot of that. Then you mix it a little, and then over the top you ripple a little Benedictine, just a little. That's the best Manhattan in the world. You can do it on the rocks or straight up chilled and it is the best either way." My eternal thanks to you Al, wherever you are, last of which was in pre-retirement in Phoenix.

Philosophy was another thing you would get at the Theatrical. Some of the best came from Nino, who in his late seventies looked like he was in his early fifties. He had a full head of curly black, slicked back hair. He was always impeccably neat in his red or black vest and he always had a story from the past to tell. I loved those tales because they made me feel like I was there when I couldn't be because I was too young, or not even alive, to go into the joint.

One of my favorites was his encomium about Indians pitching greats Bob Lemon and Early Wynn. He said they could drink a boatswain's mate under the table. "They could polish off a fifth a piece on a good night and walk out," he said. "And you wouldn't find two nicer guys and better pitchers anywhere. Early was considered mean on the mound, but when he came in here he was a prince. So was Bobby Lemon. They would come in with Jimmy Hegan, their catcher, who was a peach of a guy too. But he didn't drink. He'd sit with them and have coke. He died young of a heart attack and they just kept going on. You figure that one out." Both Lemon and Wynn died recently and had reached their late 70s.

Morrie the Maitre de was another fixture in the seventies and eighties. Built like a fireplug, he never missed a thing as it went on at the Theatrical. Anybody giving anybody else trouble soon found himself out the door. Morrie couldn't have been more than five-four, but he was a strong guy.

One time, I was sitting with a colleague, a demonstrative woman of size, and while I was sitting relaxed, she suddenly thrust her right arm my way for emphasis of her point. She caught me off guard, and I fell off the stool backward, just parallel to the floor, and all of a sudden I was up again. Morrie had caught me like a fine trapeze catcher and I was back on my seat.

Almost every night, at a certain point, around 8 p.m., the legion of night ladies would come in. Usually the same ones. They were part of the family, part of the Theatrical zoo. Among these were twins. The twins always came in with a girlfriend. They'd work single, double and triple. Mostly the action was from out of town. Most of the regulars would rather sit and drink and listen to the music. Or so it seems.

Some of the ladies had other kinds of jobs and had kids. One was a seamstress for one of our esteemed dramatic arts institutions and another ran a Burger King. Some were going to college, even getting advanced degrees. They came in different colors and sizes and they were certainly all part of the gang. I wish I could mention their names but enough people would recognize them, and besides they are probably watching their grandchildren these days.

One of the other bartenders, John, a roly-poly, happy-go-lucky guy always had late-breaking news for you when you'd come in after work. News, weather and sports. Who needed the local TV news? John was usually more accurate. And he'd have the latest jokes. He knew about trades or signings on the Indians or Cavs or Browns before they happened. He gave us the scoop on the Danny Ferry deal that brought the big guy to Cleveland for a 10-year run. A few days later the newspapers, TV and radio had the story. He was a human wire service. How did he know about these things? Maybe information passed on by a patron, maybe like the Internet, from direct links to the teams themselves.

I mentioned some of the big name musicians who were part of the Theatrical's legendary past. There were some lesser names that nonetheless fed color into this cultural mecca.

One was Glen Covington, a black pianist who amazingly played without using his thumbs. This would give most piano players a decided disadvantage, but not Covington. He was an entertainer's entertainer. He knew just about any song called from the bar or the dining room. And he was a towering figure up there on the high bandstand at the center of the Theatrical bar.

He would pack them in for years every St. Patty's day, singing "Danny Boy," and all the other Irish tunes in a brogue that sounded like it came right out of Killarney. Loudspeakers on the outside of the Theatrical would pull celebrants into the place. I'm sure the people who had never before seen Glen Covington must have thought he came from the Old Sod. They'd get a shock when they found out he was black and really a jazz man who would transmogrify each St. Patrick's day into a giant green leprechaun.

Another guy of considerable talent, a guy from the old guard of the thirties, forties and fifties who was still playing actively in the seventies and eighties was Bill Doggett. He had gotten fame first as a jazz piano player and arranger, working with titans such as Lucky Millander and Dizzy Gillespie, but was most remembered for his hit record of the late fifties, "Honky Tonk." He played the big Hammond B-3 organ for years at the Theatrical. Usually made several two-week trips there a year. He finally switched to a synthesizer, which he felt was never the same as the hefty B-3, but now in his late seventies, it was too much for him and his mates to lift. Bill wore a dark black "rug" that helped him look much younger than his years and he was still in overall good shape after all that time on the road. He had a fine tenor sax player, Bubba Brooks, in the band. Bubba often looked comatose, but when it came time to hit his notes, hit them he did. The singer for many years was a girl named Toni Williams, and she was an Aretha Franklin type whom Bill Doggett prominently featured.

Every night, though, he'd play "Honky Tonk," a piece that had gone to the top of the charts in the fifties, and people never tired of it. I wondered if Bill did, having played it tens of thousands of times. He never showed it bothered him if it did. He was one of the gentlest musicians I met at the Theatrical. And modest, too. Not many patrons knew of his extensive musical background, beyond "Honky Tonk."

Lastly, let me introduce you to Rick Hardeman, a clarinetist from New Orleans who found a regular home at the Theatrical for close to 20 years. Rick, who is still going strong in New York and also plays much in Vegas and Atlantic City, has a Benny Goodman-like voicing. It's also "New Awlins," influenced by Irving Fazola, Sydney Bechet and Pete Fountain, the latter two of whom were early influences on Fountain. Pete passed on to Rick his knowledge of the wide-bore mouthpiece technique that Fazola had passed on to him. A big, mellow, low register.

One time when I was there to hear Rick and his band, Woody Herman walked into the Theatrical, sat at a stool, heard a couple of sets and before he walked out he uttered these words, the only words he uttered all night. "Rick, you just gas me out." And that was that. Woody was appearing somewhere near Cleveland, had to make the ritual stop at the Theatrical, and found a surprise. I told Rick that might be the best compliment he'll ever receive - and this from a giant of the industry.

A lot went on at the Theatrical before and during my time. It doesn't anymore, and that is our distinct loss. It was the last of the clubs that brought people in from places like New York, Chicago, Detroit, Pittsburgh, Toledo, Columbus and St. Louis. These were people who liked to have a good time in the night. Many jazz and dining clubs in other towns, such as New York - clubs such as Toots Shor's and Jimmy Weston's - are long gone, too. People found other ways to entertain themselves. That is both good and bad. I'm glad I got to know our Theatrical Grill in its last couple of decades. And, while I couldn't get in, I'm glad I got to know it a couple of decades earlier, sitting on the curbstone.

CHAPTER
NINE

The Last Attempt to Save the Theatrical

The nails were in the coffin of the Theatrical in the early '90s. Buddy Spitz, the owner, was ready to pack it in. Crowds were thin. No longer was the main floor bustling, and the floor above, The Commerce Club, wasn't intact at all. Below, a grill-room that always was busy at lunchtime was long silent. But still operating were two large kitchens and a bakery that were second to none in the city.

Jim Swingos — who had made a notable success with his Swingos Keg & Quarter at the corner of East 18th and Euclid Avenue, and had later moved his operations to the old Statler Hotel, down the street, and still later yet, had taken over the Silver Quill on the Gold Coast, which to this day he owns and operates —was ready to take a chance on the Theatrical. He took over management of the Theatrical and tried his damnedest to revive it.

Ernie Krivda, a larger than life world-class sax player and bandleader - who earlier in his career toured the globe with the Tommy Dorsey Orchestra and Quincy Jones and has recorded dozens of delightful, thoughtful albums — and I collaborated on a jazz series at the "T." We brought in some heavy weights from all over the country to participate and record there. Among them were the gifted guitarists Gene Bertoncini, Cal Collins (who had a long association with Benny Goodman) and Joshua Breakstone; singers Kitty Margolis, Paula Owens and Roseanna Vitro; pianist Bill Dobbins and quite a few others. Sometimes we'd get a good crowd and sometimes it would be thin. Krivda, Swingos and I gave it our all with promotion and heart, but the old club just wouldn't catch again and we went on to our other endeavors.

There was a benefit to all this, though, as Ernie and I forged a strong bond. Earlier, Ernie had been based in New York for many years but decided to come back home to his roots. One of his disciples back home had been a young Joe Lovano, who today is at the peak of his powers as a sax player and regularly named in the magazine polls at the top of the list for his instrument. Another mentor, an earlier one, for Lovano was Hank Geer, a remarkable gentleman, visionary, and explorer of life itself, whom you'll meet in the next chapter.

Sometime later, Krivda was visiting with me in my office and he said he had this idea to honor Stan Getz and he wanted to do it with the Cleveland Orchestra. I encouraged him to go for the project with all of his gusto, which he did. A year and a half later he accomplished his mission, presenting Getz's great work, "Focus," with the Orchestra at Severance Hall. It had only been played one other time, by Getz, at Hunter College in New York in the early 1960s, just as Getz was becoming famous for introducing bossa nova to the United States with singer Astrud Gilberto. "Focus" was anything but bossa nova, in fact it was almost a modern classical form with jazz flavorings and, until he died, it was always Getz's favorite work, a long piece arranged by Eddie Sauter.

I was proud to see my friend, in front of an almost filled Severance Hall, flawlessly mount this work, accompanied by the full string section of the Cleveland Orchestra and other Orchestra players. I was seated in the symphony conductor's loge and when I looked to my right, I could see Getz's longtime sidemen, the bassist Rufus Reid and the pianist Andy LaVerne, entranced in another loge. They had opened the show with Ernie, playing the standard Getz repertoire, including bossa. Appearing with them in the first half was the drummer, another Getz stalwart, Adam Nussbaum. He joined Ernie and the Orchestra for the second half presentation of "Focus."

All of which is to say that the waning days of the Theatrical had their merits. Ernie and I often talked of musical ideas there and some of them led to good things that happened later. Maybe the great ghosts inside the walls of the Theatrical had something to do with this inspiration.

Today, Ernie enjoys continued success with his much-recorded Fat Tuesday Big Band, a 17-piece ensemble that plays every Tuesday night at the Savannah Bar & Grill in Westlake. They recently shared the stage before a full house at the State Theater with Gregory Hines. And he shines with his other groups, trios, quartets and quintets. He is a Cleveland treasure who once, when he led the house band at the Smiling Dog Saloon on Cleveland's near West Side, was asked by headliner Miles Davis if he would join Davis on his international tours, as his lead sax player. Ernie demurred, because, at the time, he didn't like the fusion music Davis was playing. He has always been a man of his own mind. A Cleveland original.

At the time, Ernie and his colleagues were playing some funky stuff of their own with bop innovator and Cleveland guitarist Bill De Arango, who had earlier been a major collaborator with Charlie Parker and Dizzy Gillespie in New York. In the mid-70s they were playing a discordant, multi-keyed jazz that as Ernie said, "We thought it was real cool at the time. We had at least two of every instrument, including two drummers, and everyone was playing in different keys and rhythms. Some people really got off on this, although I'm not sure anyone understood what we were doing, including sometimes us. It was, pure and simple, free jazz. Some time later we listened to the recordings we did at the Smiling Dog, and most of us, except for perhaps Bill De Arango, thought they were more than a little weird. We decided to go off into other musical directions. But I got a good musical education down there off of West 25th Street at the Smiling Dog."

Indeed he did, sharing the stage with Gillespie, James Moody, Phil Woods, Getz, Gerry Mulligan and a host of other icons that influenced his music.

CHAPTER
TEN

Meet Mr. Henry Gerspacher

A number of the people you are meeting in this book are musicians or at least musically inclined, but this is not just a book about music and sports from a Cleveland angle. No, this is about the interesting souls, past and present, who have made and are still making this a place that is both cultural, soothing and provocative. To me, they all have been inimitable.

No one fit this bill better than Hank Geer, who left us for a whole new world in November of 2000.

His non-stage name was Henry Gerspacher, a product of Collinwood, vintage 1922. He was the sweetest and smartest man I have had the pleasure of knowing. He also had the toughness of Job.

About ten years ago, 'round about midnight, Hank Geer was standing out on the deck of Sammy's Restaurant on Old River Road in the Flats looking at the march of boats going up and down the Cuyahoga, listening to the revelers on the west bank, looking up at the stars and the bridges. Suddenly, an over-served motorist swung into the small parking area next to Sammy's and plowed into the deck, hurtling Hank over the railing and down a slope to the road below, about a 15-foot drop. By the time startled onlookers and Sammy's workers could get to him, Hank had gotten himself up and was brushing himself off. They asked him to sit down, that they would call an ambulance. And he emphatically said no. He had another set to play and it was time to get back. They prevailed, and he was on his way to Metro General Hospital, where the doctors told him he had a broken left arm, a mangled hand, a broken pelvis, a bad concussion and an assortment of other injuries, that he was lucky he wasn't killed. They said they would have to operate. Hank, who at one time had been a med student, said, "Well, then, let's do it . . . make me better than I am right now and that will be just fine with me!"

Just on the sunny side of 70, Hank was to have a long trail ahead of him for recuperation and rehabilitation. How someone so innocently could have been injured and almost eliminated was nothing that bothered Hank. In the months that followed, he never uttered one verbal shot at the other guy, the miscreant driver, though his legion of friends couldn't have been said to have been as mild reacting. They all adored Hank and hated to see him suffer and go through the rigors of getting his health back.

Not Hank. He figured this was just another challenge to surmount in a lifetime of challenges that saw him mostly succeed where many others would have given up.

In rehab, some very good doctors at University Hospitals tended to him. These guys knew who he was and they wanted to get him back to playing his horn as quickly as they could. They included orthopedic and hand specialists. There was one other thing, these guys were all frustrated musicians, fans of Hank's, and they leapt to be on the team that put Hank back together again.

Less than a year later, he was back on the little bandstand at Sammy's, playing his alto and soprano saxes. His quintet, "Jazz Alive," was reunited. Hank's left arm and hand had been so damaged that initially it was thought that he would never regain the use of them. But he did, because Hank Geer wouldn't give up. In fact, he improved so much that he also was able to begin playing the piano again. This was important because most any singer who has sung with Hank, preferred him to be her accompanist than anyone else. He could block out chords better than anyone and he stayed right with them, even when they trailed off key. He was a musician's musician. His longest-running chanteuse was Marilyn Holderfield. She appeared with Hank for the better of the 20 years he made Sammy's his home. Marilyn, who still sings in Key West, Florida, has a Helen Merrill, Chris Connor, Anita O'Day sort of jazzy, sultry voice. She and Hank always made good music together. As did his regular sidemen, Frankie Daniels on piano, Dick Meese on base, and Archie Frane, on drums.

Business at Sammy's picked up when Hank came back, and for the life of me I could never figure out which came first, Hank or Sammy's. Certainly, Hank had as much to do with creating the atmosphere there as the quaint, wood-beamed and windowed room itself did. Sammy's had so much popularity in its first decade, from 1981-91, that it was named one of Esquire magazine's "Ten Best Watering Holes In America." The presence of Hank and his band had a lot to do with that, I'm sure. They played "hot, sophisticated jazz," the words Marilyn used to sign off each of their sets for "Jazz Alive." The food at Sammy's was also among the best you could get in our part of the country. The wait staff was wonderful, and some of us in the dining room were often served by a young Drew Carey, just beginning his way up the hill in comedy.

Marilyn and I and a few others would frequently traipse over to the old Cleveland Comedy Club to watch him stretch out his material in those days. After his gig at Sammy's, he'd frequently appear at the Comedy Club, usually the last act, when the headliner typically was someone like Jay Leno. Those were fun days, back in the early and mid 1980s.

One of Carey's main shticks at the time was to wear a black, hinged tie and white shirt, along with a business suit and his identifying black-rimmed glasses. After he'd done a number of jokes, he would do impressions, such as "man in the wind," "man on the go," "man running away from mad husband." Then he would jack up his tie so that it was horizontal to the ground, giving the impression that he was a man in a hurry. It was not too long afterward that Carey began playing dates out of town and he himself became a headliner, did the Carson show and the rest is the Drew Carey we know and love today.

"Drew Carey hasn't changed one bit from the time he worked at Sammy's," says Holderfield. "In fact, the part he plays on his TV show is every bit him. We had a goofy crew back then and I loved every minute of it."

However, if there were one supreme allied commander of all things at Sammy's it was Hank Geer.

· · ·

I first met Hank in 1981, when Sammy's had just opened. It's first few months it was just a bar, then it became a full-service gourmet restaurant. The band then played at the far wall on the south side of the big, two-decked dining room.

I was having dinner with friends one night, and my ears perked up at the music. It had a sweet, mainstream jazz sound, with good rhythm. I first noticed Marilyn Holderfield singing. She is tall and blonde and at that time her hair was cut very short. She has big blue eyes, fluttering eyelashes and a great voice, a voice from gone by. She had been a housewife and mother for many years and decided she wanted to augment her life. With a tremendous affinity to remember the words to songs, she just started singing those words. Hank once told me he liked her immediately, saying "Marilyn was just a natural. I have had some really good singers in my time, but she was one who just knew how to hit the notes without trying too hard."

That night was the first night I had ever seen Hank Geer. Now this guy looked like a jazz guy right out of the thirties and forties, and in fact he was a jazz guy from that era. When I first saw him he was in his late fifties, and he was just beginning a nearly two-decade gig at the restaurant, six nights a week.

Hank was a trim but sturdy man of about five-nine. The crescent that was his remaining hair was shaved to the skin and on top of that bald head sat his trademark, a black beret, slanted just so slightly. He also wore a whitish beard. The quintessential jazzman.

He had a pinkish complexion, made more pink when he played his horn, usually the alto sax. His blue eyes bulged out as he'd hit crescendos. His music was good to the ear, ever-present but not intrusive in the dining room.

Some time later, Sammy's moved the bandstand from the back of the dining room to a corner spot next to the long "L"-shaped bar. This was a better spot and it made the bar all the livelier. And between breaks and frequently after the last set, I got to know Hank as not only a renaissance man but also a pundit and philosopher of considerable magnitude. Over the twenty years that I knew him, I was to receive an education on many topics, not the least of which was music.

Hank was able to play any instrument. He'd been doing that since he was a precocious youngster. Listening to records and picking up the tones to play on the piano. His sister Bertha, a few years his senior, says, "He picked up any instrument and could play it almost immediately. But after he fooled around with it, he would find out how to really play it. He was always very serious about studying music. He was playing in bands before he was a teenager. His whole life was music but Henry knew a lot more than that."

I learned - not from him, of course - that Hank played trumpet, piccolo, all the saxes, standup bass, trombone, guitar, violin, etc. Probably his favorite instruments were the alto and soprano saxophones. These were the instruments that were his signature at Sammy's. He also was outstanding on the piano and in his later years at Sammy's, when he was having some lip problems, he pretty much stuck to that. Hearing him play just with a bassist, Dick Meese, Chink Stephenson or Dallas Coffey, for example, the voicings were wonderful.

But there are those who say Hank was at his best on the Hammond B-3 organ, which he played at a place he owned called the Shore Club. It was on Lakeshore Boulevard, near Nothingham Road. There, he would entertain nightly. Often the sidemen turned out to be touring musicians such as the legendary drummer Gene Krupa. Ernie Krivda and Joe Lovano got their early starts in jazz there, as did many other Cleveland musicians of their generation. Hank was the master and the mentor. He inspired with positive reinforcement. He never was known to utter a cross word.

During that time, he also came up with a dynamic idea called the "Six Saxophones." This was a band that featured the six different instruments in the saxophone family playing at once, backed with a rhythm section of piano, base and drums. Hank found guys to play the bass saxophone, the baritone, the tenor, the alto, the soprano, and the tiny piccolo sax. Much of their efforts were recorded and Hank gave me a variety of these selections on tape. The sound was that of a 17-piece big jazz band but mellower and distinctly its own. Like a Miles Davis, Hank Geer was always innovating and experimenting throughout his life.

He recorded a great deal of his work over the different eras, especially the band and singers at Sammy's. My hope is someone will take this repertoire and make it available to more people, especially musicians and budding youngsters who are just getting into the field. Hank was a notable teacher and what he taught to musicians and other people was stuff to be absorbed and treasured.

CHAPTER ELEVEN

The Mentor, The Master

"Ronnie, you know there is so much out there, so much more than we know as humans," Hank Geer mused one night.

"I love it here at Sammy's because those big windows let us see all the stars on a clear night. Man, there is so much out there. We just know the tip of it."

Indeed, the place in which we were conversing had a "look." It was a one-of-a-kind place, Sammy's. The main restaurant is closed now, used for private parties, as are the other parts of the large building on Old River Road. The owners, Ralph DiOrio and Denise Fugo, figured that their catering business was the better part of valor and it was time to close the restaurant as we knew it and tend to catering there and at other locations they run. Who can blame them? Instead, I commend them, and their original partners Sammy Catania and his wife Roberta, for opening it in the first place and providing me a classroom of twenty years of graduate studies, taught by Professor Henry Gerspacher, aka Hank Geer.

Hank loved the bridges over and around the Cuyahoga. After they lit up some of them in different colors for the Cleveland bicentennial, he became even more animated about them. One night I said I thought the Detroit-Superior Bridge had been gerry-built. I thought the bridge looked funny, with its outside lanes outside the superstructure above, as if they were appended as an afterthought. The superstructure itself seemed too short for the underbody below, which carried the old electric streetcars across the river to the West Side. I took a number of trips across the Cuyahoga with my father Archie when I was a little lad. It was frightening looking down where you would see nothing but air and the Cuyahoga some 100 feet below. Some years later they had sealed off the streetcar lanes. The Detroit-Superior's majestic concrete arches supporting the bridge on land and encasing the streetcar tracks, I thought, were the best part of the bridge. Hank agreed, but overall he said the bridge "was meant to be built the way it looked." He said, "That's how it doesn't fall down. It is self supporting at the center, over water." And then he went on to give me a deep lecture on the physics of bridge building, from the Golden Gate to the Rainbow Bridge to the London Bridge back to the Detroit-Superior. And I felt better with this new knowledge.

• • •

Hank was an avid skier and he helped make Ellicottville, New York, the Aspen of the East. The little hamlet, located about 90 miles southeast of Buffalo, was a sleepy little place until the late 1950s when Hank and friends started skiing there. Today it is a year-around recreational area and its skiing especially is the best to be had between the Rockies and Vermont. When Hank was skiing he was also playing music there at the Bird Walk and the Silver Fox at night.

In addition, Hank was a building owner and developer in Cleveland and Ellicottville and he had a farm in southern Ohio. He always had something going on, his hands in many pots.

When Hank graduated from Miami University in Oxford in the mid-1940s, he headed for medical school in Cincinnati. He had always wanted to be a doctor and went forward with that plan until the muse of music was just too much to overcome. He played in the house band at WLW-Radio in the Queen City when a young Doris Day was a singer there. Later he moved to Tucson and also spent a good deal of time in Los Angeles where the West Coast jazz scene was just starting to happen. He spent plenty of time in New York playing in the 52nd Street clubs on stages that presented the likes of Dizzy Gillespie, Charlie Parker, Erroll Garner, Eddie Condon, Roy Eldridge, Vic Dickerson and Benny Carter. He was one of them and he never let go of the hipster lingo that musicians of that era had in their vernacular.

When the night was done and it was time to say goodbye, Hank would always intone, "In a minute, Ronnie. In a minute." "In a minute, Hank," I would reply.

To Hank, good people were "Cats." "That guy is one good Cat," Hank would say. "What did you think of the Cats who came in tonight?" he would ask after one of the Friday night jam sessions at Sammy's. Hank was a veritable magnet for musicians, good musicians, all of whom had professional backgrounds.

Some of these guys - by now they were pretty much all in their seventies — played under Hank's leadership in the Campus Owls band at Miami.   In fact, in his later years he re-organized the Campus Owls for annual reunions.   They always played at the time of graduation in June and the kids of a much younger generation could see what it must have been like when the Owls were in their heyday from the 1920s through the 1950s.   Many of the guys went on to be professional musicians, some had dual careers in medicine, law and engineering.

Hank was always proud of the fact that the 17-piece Campus Owls band would go up against the respected professional bands of the day, such as Ray Anthony, and beat their butts sometimes in battle of the bands competition.   "We were considered a school swing band and we were supposed to be amateurs, but everyone in the group made real good money in those days because we played many events and in the summer, Christmas time and during spring break, we'd tour," Hank would reminisce.   They even made two European tours.

I got to meet a number of these guys, certainly all the ones from the Cleveland area.   And when people from other cities came into town, they'd always head down to Sammy's to sit in on the Friday jam sessions.   So I met a lot of Hank's old friends. And I watched as one-by-one they dropped off and I could see the sadness in Hank's eyes.

After Marilyn Holderfield left Hank's "Jazz Alive" group after more than 15 years at Sammy's, Hank would feature other singers on different nights.   He nurtured them and helped them gain the confidence they needed to reach new heights in their work.   He was very patient, even when things would go wrong. Someone might sing off key or forget the words, and Hank, playing the piano or alto sax, would vamp for them. The audience was never the wiser.

Two singers who applaud Hank for his encouragement over the years at Sammy's and at other venues, Sue Hesse and Evelyn Wright, can't say enough about his mentorship. Both now are extremely popular singers in Cleveland.

At the time of Hank's death in November of 2000, Evelyn Wright and I walked out of the funeral home in Euclid and just looked at each other. We were unable to speak because of our mutual feeling of deep loss. Later, Evelyn, said, "That man meant everything to me and a lot of other people in and out of the music business. He was the most even-tempered gentleman. I never heard him say a harsh word about anyone." I agreed, stating that when you were around Hank something mystical happened.

Sitting at Sammy's just a couple of years ago, Hank said to me, "Ronnie, you know there is so much more out there that we don't understand. This is just one life and around it there is so much mystery." We didn't talk about religion per se, not in a traditional or organized way, but in my mind Hank Geer was a deeply religious person who was sincerely thankful for the many personal gifts he possessed. He never wanted to waste them.

In the last months of his life, Hank was in pretty bad shape. I called him from Morton's one afternoon and said I'd like to visit him at Lutheran Medical Center. He was happy that I called but he said that I should call again before I came out because he was receiving therapy and they would take him out of his room at different times of the day. On the phone, I said, "Hank, I just want you to know how much you mean to me and how much I love you." He didn't want me to come out for nothing. The point here is that as sick as he was with cancer, which had reached his brain, he was gung-ho about his therapy, just as he was a decade earlier after the car accident that nearly killed him.

By this time, he had had his right leg amputated because of infections and gangrene that had set in.

When I walked into his room the next day, he was the old Hank that I knew and loved. His stolid older sister Bertha was there as well. We talked freely. Hank told me some fascinating stories and as he told them, the stump of his right leg would thump up and down for emphasis, or as if he were tapping the beat to a music only he could hear.

Hank had been pretty well doped up prior to reaching the hospital. For a number of weeks he had been in a nursing home. He related the experience, and sometimes Bertha would shake her head and sometimes she and I would burst out laughing.

"Ronnie, I can't tell what it was like exactly, but when they had me on whatever they had me on I went out of my head," Hank recalled. "It was crazy, man. Those Cats gave me some real hard stuff and for a while I didn't know where I was. But then for a while I was on this long trip to different places. I was in Peru, I went to Puerto Rico, to Lima, Ohio. And it wouldn't end. I couldn't stop it. I used to like to travel but on this trip I just kept going to these weird places, some I had never been to before. It was fun for a while but then I couldn't get off the bus. The next thing I knew is that I woke up in this hospital room and I felt better. Bertha said, "I think he got better once they got him off this stuff. He seemed to come back to earth."

At Lutheran, Hank had streams of visitors. When I walked up to the reception desk, I said I'd like to see Hank... I didn't even utter his last name. The desk clerk knew immediately whom I was there to see.

Many of us who had seen Hank at the hospital at different times compared notes. All of us said that he had entertained us with his stories. I know the day I was there, he was sharp as a tack. Bertha talked of having him wheeled down the hall to play the piano, which would have been good for Hank and many other "guests" of the hospital in varying states of malady. I'm not sure that plan ever happened, because it wasn't long after that I got the call that Hank had died.

Now if you have to die, you should have a send off like Hank did. It was a three-day affair, with live music, even at the funeral home, especially at the funeral home. Hank was decked out in a strikingly red blazer with black flocking and black buttons. Of course on his head, at a jaunty angle, was his trademark beret. He looked good. He looked like the Hank of his prime.

Musicians, relatives, friends, neighbors - hundreds of people of all walks of life, religious persuasions, races - were there. They were asked to tell Hank stories, and many of them did. How much he meant to them or some anecdotal happening about Hank. Most of these stories were warm and joyous and some hilarious. I wanted to say something but I couldn't at that time. Nor could Evelyn Wright. And when the testimonials were over, the band again returned for another set.

I just wrote in the attendance book. "In a minute, Hank. With all my love and thanks."

If you haven't heard Hank's band, "Jazz Alive," you still can, minus the maestro, but still very good indeed. They play on Wednesday nights and for Sunday brunch at Swingos' Silver Quill in the Carlyle in Lakewood.

The players include the bassist Dick Meese, drummer Archie Frane, Frankie Daniels on the piano, Buddy Sullivan on tenor sax, and the one-and-only Evelyn Wright on vocals. Hank I'm sure is happy that "Jazz Alive" is still alive.

We all miss him but to most of us who knew Hank well his presence has had a life-long impression. No one who knew him will ever forget Henry Gerspacher.

CHAPTER
TWELVE

Dark Eyes

I met this Lebanese-Syrian-American girl in the summer of 1973. I almost didn't meet her as well. We met in August and were married the following December. That was almost 28 years ago. When I met her all of her life-long friends were married and had children. I felt like an oddball because I was divorced. I thought I wasn't like them. There were about six of us couples. I wasn't sure I fit in. Now, all of those perfect couples are divorced and I'm still married to the little girl with beautiful dark eyes. Life is strange, and I'm damned lucky.

As I looked across the long back room of the "Last Moving Picture Company" on Euclid at Playhouse Square, I saw this woman who absolutely stepped out of the crowd. Must have been 300 people there, sitting around large round tables at this once popular Cleveland eatery. They were there to see the premiere of the fall programming for Channel 61, the old TV station. I had just come off a two-week road trip and was exhausted. I had just spent two weeks with a client, and that is hard for anyone to do. You need some space, but this guy insisted we attend the party for Channel 61. And so I went, reluctantly.

My client disappeared somewhere into the crowd in search of a drink. I just stood around looking at the new shows featured on the screen and then I spotted her. She had an absolutely gorgeous profile, aquiline nose, with big dark, doe-like eyes. A good chin and high cheekbones. Her hair was very dark brown, curly and set in a shag. I couldn't keep my eyes off her.

After the show, I couldn't find my client. I figured I'd go to the bar, have a drink, and he would eventually show up, since I drove.

I was staring at the back of the bar, really getting relaxed, when I noticed a presence to my right. It was the girl from the center of the room that I had admired from afar. She was seated right next to me. We started to talk and that conversation is still going 28 years later. What a stroke of luck.

You know when you hit it off with the right girl. And that we did. Just about the time that we were going to go to another location for a bite to eat, my client returned and pronounced that it was now time to leave. He had disappeared for such a long time I thought that maybe he had found another way home. But there he was and he thought it was time to go. I said I wasn't ready just yet. Since he never carried money with him - I picked up all the tabs for both of us - I gave him ten bucks for a cab. He took that the wrong way, as if I were trying to drop kick him, my big client. His nostrils flared, steam may have come out of his ears and he did an about face out the door. Turns out he exchanged nine cents for a dime from someone on Euclid Avenue and called his wife to pick him up. We didn't talk for two weeks, my client who represented the biggest account at my agency. I didn't give a damn. I had more important things on my mind than being a babysitter.

Her name was Simona Yesbak and she was with the Marschalk Company, a large Cleveland ad agency. I'd been splitting my time between New York and Toledo at the time working on various accounts, traveling constantly around the country, for another agency. Cleveland was a test market for the big client that I mentioned, so I found myself spending a good deal of time in my old hometown, which was fine with me. It was just a pure coincidence, though, that I met Simona. I came very close to pulling the plug on that station party and taking a plane back to New York.

I'm glad Simona seemed to like me just as much as I was fond of her. Through her I learned more than a little something about Arabic culture, especially their splendid food and their deep sense of family. At the time she was 27, never married, and I was 29 and getting a divorce. Looking back, that seems so young by today's standards. We couldn't get married in the church because the Catholics, which she was, wouldn't allow a marriage between a woman and a divorced man, though I too was Catholic. So on December 21st of 1973 we got married by the Lakewood municipal judge in my wife's sister's house, surrounded by her abundant family, all of them of Lebanese or Syrian descent or both. Besides the chance meeting on August 7th of that year, the best day of my life was December 21st. I put Simona right at the head of the pack of the remarkable people I have mentioned earlier and the other special Cleveland people I will tell you about later.

It is considerable to understand the scope of Cleveland ethnicity and to realize what we have here. Too often, we take all this for granted, and one purpose of writing *A Love Story For Cleveland* is that by reading my own story, you might realize your own. Through this journey of some six decades, I hope we both will become richer in memories and the appreciation for what we have today in a good town with good people. If you aren't from Cleveland but have spent time here or have moved here, maybe the book will demonstrate what we have here. This has certainly happened for me in telling these stories.

Simona and her older sister Lee are very close. They talk to each other every morning, without fail. They sound identical, and when you pick up an extension phone by accident you can't tell which one of these sisters is speaking. They are very close for many reasons, the biggest of which is forged by the fact that they are orphans. Their mother, Ida, died first, about a year after Simona was born. Their father, Simon, died several years later of pure and simple anguish over his loss. I would have given anything to have known them. To have two such beautiful, caring, family-centric daughters, you know the parents had to be special too.

Their aunt, Frances Nassif, who had four children of her own, raised the girls. Her husband, John, get this, was the headwaiter at the Theatrical Grill, the famed emporium depicted with relish earlier. For some reason the Theatrical has had a mysticism for me most of my life. My first office when I started my own agency was directly across the street from the "T" in the old National City Bank Building. I could see it from my window on the 5th floor.

So while I was sitting around on the curbstone in front of the Theatrical when I was 16 or 17, it turns out Simona was probably inside having dinner with her family.

The Nassif family and Simona and Lee grew up in a nice big house on Lake Avenue in Cleveland, after starting out in the old West 14th Street area, Tremont, where many of the Arabic families lived from before the turn of the 20th century. Lee and Simona were born in the Greensburg-Latrobe area in the lush and rolling Laurel Valley region of Pennsylvania. If their parents had lived, chances are they still would be there where many of the mother's family still live.

Frances did a good job of raising the Yesbak kids. The name, by the way, was really Yezbak, but their father Simon wanted to "Americanize" the name. He had gone to Georgetown and then got a job with National Cash Register as a regional salesman and had later become a sales manager. He had done well - until the death of his wife, Ida. Ida was darkly pretty and Sy looked like Humphrey Bogart. The pictures I have seen many times show a beautiful couple. I truly wish I could have known them and that my wife could have enjoyed her parents for many years and that they could have enjoyed our children. Simona has made a sterling mother of herself because she treasures having a closeness with our kids and my two children from my first marriage. I feel for her that she did not get to know her own parents.

People often ask how Simona was given such a beautiful name. The answer is simple. After their first daughter, Ida and Simon, especially Simon, were expecting a son, Simon Jr. So they ingeniously came up with the unusual name of Simona when they got another baby girl.

Simona is cautious and I'm a risk-taker. That has been a good combination of balance. But it is also a good combination of combat. We have probably had on average an argument a day, starting from the first night we met. But we get over it fast and go on. We communicate, and I think that is what has held us together for so long.

She and I like many of the same things, so overall we get along very well. We both share a respect for our ethnic backgrounds and have enjoyed exploring them.

As an only child with a very small family, I have enjoyed the largeness of the Lebanese-Syrian clan. Among them are Yesbaks, Nassifs and Maroons. They are all hearty, loving people with, certainly, the matriarch at the center of it all. When the matriarch reaches about 55, they begin to call her "Sittu," which means grandmother in English.

My wife's aunt, Frances, was the Sittu of Sittues. She was smart as a whip and no one would ever dare cross her. She was worshipped and treated like a queen, and she deserved every bit of it.

When I showed up one night for the first time with Simona, her aunt looked askance. She wondered who was this guy with the brown-checkered, double-vented suit and clog-like shoes with high heels? This was 1973 and I was in fashion, but I'm sure not to her. The only word she said to me was "hello." And that was it. No "goodbye, good to see you, or anything else." Later, Simona told me her aunt really liked me. I knew her for 25 years until her death at 92, and we really never had a conversation but I respected her intelligence and her intuition and, besides, I knew she really liked me because she knew that I would never let down her niece. Sittu was someone who loved and was loved by all around her. Her dark eyes glistened with alertness and her face was physically beautiful until she died. Not a wrinkle, truly.

It was through the loving cooking of Sittu that I learned the wonderfulness of Lebanese food. This is the best food there is, and it's good for you too. Tibuli, hummus, fatoya, grape leaves, raw and cooked kibbi and single-layer pita bread were all different from the Slovenian blood and rice sausage, the cornmeal and Vienna bread I grew up with. Single-layer pita bread is much different and much better than the double-layer pita that you buy in the store, and it takes hours to make. Very few calories and very elastic and tasty with the various Lebanese dishes.

The only trouble with raw kibbi, which is ground lamb meat similar to a steak tartare but better, is that the next day you might feel like you swallowed a bowling ball. But it's delicious the night before.

The gatherings of the big Lebanese and Syrian family are always happenings. Almost everyone in Simona's family has mucho kids, and as the younger generation has its own kids, the group gets bigger and bigger. Fifty people come in the door to our home and fifty-six people leave. They seem to multiply like the schmooes of the Lil' Abner cartoon series. You have to love these people. They are American, mind you, but they have not lost one bit of their Middle Eastern heritage. That's what I like about my town.

To think that these different heritages — mine being one half Slovenian, one quarter Scottish and one quarter Swiss and blending that with Simona's Lebanese-Syrian background — could mix or would even find one another is quite astounding. I can't think of another city on earth, with perhaps the exception of Chicago, where this could readily happen. When you think that Cleveland has at least 70 different ethnicities in its metropolitan area, the permutations of these possible combinations is even more astonishing. I love it. And I'm proud that it happens here, and you should be as well. We are Americans for sure, but America stands for exactly what the melting pot of Cleveland represents. May it always be so.

. . .

Simona and I share a love for the game of baseball. We were lucky enough to have had a front row seat at Opening Day in 1975 when Frank Robinson became the first black manager in baseball history. His first time up in that first game he hit a homerun. What a thrill. Here was a guy who had been MVP in both leagues before he came to Cleveland. One of the greatest players of all time. And we had him now as a player-manager, which hadn't been done since Lou Boudreau managed the Tribe in the 1940s.

That same year we were at another game, a night game, when the Great Walenda tight-roped his way from right field to left field. That would be across the field from the right field roof to the left field roof, standing on his head in the middle for dramatic appeal. He was at least ten stories above the ground, without a net. At the time, the Great Walenda was in his seventies.

People asked how he could do this, and he answered that he always got himself nice and relaxed by having two extra dry martinis before performing. I remember many things about the old ballpark. This could be the highlight and it had nothing to do with baseball or football.

Many years later Simona and I had seats on the field for the celebration dedicating the opening of the Rock and Roll Hall of Fame and Museum. It was an awe-inspiring sight, not just because of Bob Dylan, Bruce Springsteen, Chuck Berry, Mary Wilson, the Allman Brothers Band and many other stars, but also because, to me, there was the premonition that this was the last really big event that ever would take place there. That same fall the Browns announced that they were leaving town. The team was not very good then, so the really last crowning glory for Municipal Stadium was the Rock Hall event.

Our seats were on the grass out in center-right field. The stage was set against the bleachers, so when I turned around I could see this mass of humanity in the horseshoe of the upper and lower decks, and somehow I knew that this was it for the old lady. The sports center of gravity was then switching to Gateway and Jacobs Field and she had had it. I was very sad.

One time at the old Stadium Club at Municipal in the early nineties Art Modell was having a party to announce the need to rehab Municipal or to build a new stadium. A big crowd was on hand, and I remember Modell hugging Ozzie Newsome, his long-time tight end and now Hall of Famer. Ozzie obviously agreed with Art that we needed a new park. I was standing next to one of the city's ranking luminaries and said to him, "You know, I like this old stadium. I have so many memories here . . . the Indians, Jimmy Brown, Bobby Mitchell, Otto, the boxing matches, the Senate League high school championship football games, the Great Wallenda . . ." The dick looks at me like I had lost my mind. "Oh, come on," he said, "you can't be serious." I was.

I liked the old Stadium because of the memories and its user-friendliness. It was home. Jacobs Field is wonderful, and I am happy that we have a separate baseball field.

But at the first exhibition game at the new Cleveland Browns Stadium in 1999, Simona and I and our son Ronnie and daughter Mandy settled into our new seats. We were on about the ten-yard line on the northeast side. We remarked that we were indeed much closer to the field than our long-time 45-yard-line seats at the old stadium, almost too close.

The new Browns were, as expected, a dull shambles. The latest godsend, linebacker Chris Spielman, got hurt and was never to play football again. We got the notion that Chris Palmer, the head coach was B-O-R-I-N-G, and we had the most fun watching revelers in the Dawg Pound evade the massive security forces that were part of the new regime.

Somewhere in the first quarter my son and I looked at each other and said, in spite of all the gimmicks and advertising blasting away at us, and the striking orange and brown hues of Browns Stadium, the place lacked character. I know the johns are a damned sight better, but there is something about the place that lacks the gridiron grit of old Municipal. It seems like a better place to watch outdoor hai lai or perhaps a garden show. Somehow you can't imagine Jimmy Brown nailing down a nine-yard gain there and getting all dirty on the skin of the infield when he hit the ground. I don't think Otto Graham or Dante Lavelli would have enjoyed playing there. And I don't see "The Toe" knockin' one over the goal post from the 48 either. However, if you like watching commercials this is a good place to be.

We have a new stadium, but I'm glad I still have the same old wife, Simona, and she and I have enjoyed all these years together in the town of our choice.

CHAPTER
THIRTEEN

Funny People

One of the reasons I have enjoyed Cleveland so much is that it has spawned so many funny people. Truly hilarious people. Some of them might not know that they're funny but that doesn't matter. Part of this comes from the cross cultures of ethnicity. Some the specific cultures, such as the Irish.

Two of the funniest people I know made it big in Hollywood. They're both from Cleveland and they're both Irish. The first I'll mention is Jack Riley, who grew up in Lakewood, and the other is Pat McCormick, who grew up not faraway in Rocky River.

In the early 1960s Jack had a fabulously successful radio show on WERE called "Baxter & Riley." Jack's partner on the show was the basso-voiced Jeff Baxter. Their afternoon drive-time program had people rolling around with laughter in their cars. People would look out their car windows, breaking up about the same shtick. Tears would be running down their cheeks, that's how funny the guys were.

"But the real people who called in or visited the show, however inadvertently, made it even funnier," said Riley.

"We used to do a Saturday morning program at the big Sears store on Carnegie Avenue. That store is now part of the Cleveland Play House complex. But in the sixties the place was the place to go for just about anything. And people did. While Jeff and I were trying to do our show from a desk on the main floor, a guy would come up and ask us - right in the middle of the show - where the fertilizer was. Another guy would ask about the hatchets. A fat woman would pester us about the girdles. Two little kids would stand there crying with chocolate ice cream all over their faces and scream for the bathroom. We just ran with what was happening."

One of the characters Riley concocted on his drive-time show was a fellow named Gates Mills. He also would do this same character on Ernie ("Ghoulardi") Anderson's TV show along with Tom Conway, who became "Tim" Conway, a product of Chagrin Falls.

Gates Mills would talk out of the left side of his mouth as they do at the Hunt Club and in the Brahmin-influenced villages of New England. Even on radio you could see Gates' cocked but floppy checkered hat, his bow tie, his buttoned-down blue oxford and his hounds tooth jacket. Riley had this guy down to a science, and people in the audience would reel with laughter. Probably a lot of the people who talked that way never heard the show because they were too busy at the Hunt

Club or some other club they belonged too. Many of these people's fortunes had been made from the hard work of previous generations and they had it made and were sort of oblivious to the many other things, besides their lives, that were going on in Cleveland and the rest of the planet.

From the side of his mouth, Gates Mills would say something like, "Got a couple a quail early this mornnnn-ing. Got 'em with seven shots and I didn't fall off Spoonsie, my horse, when his left leg got into some quicksand in the norrrrth forrrrrrty. Must be gettin' better in my old age."

Riley followed Tim Conway to Hollywood in the mid-sixties, and, like Conway, who starred in the TV comedy series, "McHale's Navy," and went on to greater success in the movies and especially as a co-star of the "Carol Burnett Show" along with Harvey Korman, Jack soon found work.

A graduate of St. Ignatius High and John Carroll University but a guy who grew up modestly in a big family on Westwood Avenue between Detroit and Franklin in Lakewood, Jack first became nationally known playing the "Mr. Carlin" character on the original "Bob Newhart" TV show. He played the dark-haired guy who was the most neurotic and the meanest of psychologist Newhart's patients.

Jack and I were standing outside the Biltmore Hotel in downtown Los Angeles one night shortly after the Newhart show had gone off the air after a good six-year run, and some guy came waddling up to him saying, "Hey, Carleton the doorman, can I have your autograph?" The guy had Riley's Mr. Carlin character mixed up with a character from another show whose name was "Carleton the doorman."

"Such is fame," muttered Riley after he gave the guy his autograph.

Following Newhart, Jack Riley went on to become one of the top voice-over announcers for national and regional commercials and continued to do TV shows and movies. He has been a particular favorite of producer/directors such as Robert Altman and Mel Brooks. Riley had a great role in Brooks' "A Silent Movie," playing, what else, a neurotic assistant on the movie where the only person who had a speaking part is the famed mime Marcel Marceau.

Riley also had a key role in the movie, "Attack of the Killer Tomatoes," a campy cult film where there was almost a tragedy. While riding in a helicopter, trying to quell the killer tomatoes in his role as an investigator, something went wrong with the chopper and it crashed into the tomato field. Jack then said, "That's the first time actors have been thrown at tomatoes."

These days Jack continues to do voice-overs and he is a favorite of Jay Leno for bits on the "Tonight Show."

I got to know Jack in the 1970s when I asked him to be the keynote speaker at the annual conference of the American Industrial Hygiene Association. For several years I had heard one bad and boring speaker after the other at the black-tie keynote dinner, this after witnessing the delivery of several hundred technical papers on industrial hygiene, safety and occupational health topics over five previous days. I was the public relations agent for the association and for its annual conference. I convinced the executive director that on the last night when we had all 2000 industrial hygienists and their spouses together for the dinner we should have something more entertaining than Dr. Karlos

Kofmanis talking about: "The ideal epidemiological configuration
of the universe based on the impact of non-iodizing radiation."
Kofmanis had spoken the year earlier and started the drudgery by
saying something like this, in a Dracula sort of voice: "Goood
even-ing to one and to all, I am Dr. Karlos Kofmanis and I vill talk
vith you about zee very frightening aspects of non-ionizing radiation. I know you have had a long veek here at zee Biltmore in Los
Angel-eese and so I vant to keep my talk very, very short - justa
twenty meenutes and vhen twenty meenutes arrive you vill know
that Karlos Kofmanis eeze a liar." That was the funniest thing he
said that night and it went down from there and he went on for
more than an hour, with most of the audience in slumberland.

Well, Jack was a fine rebound from Dr. Kofmanis. He
got me together with Pat McCormick and Bill Larkin, a guy who
was Bob Hope's head writer for many years and did many other
shows such as "Donnie & Marie, and himself to work out a kind
of send-up of the industrial hygiene conference. I fed them straight
material about the week-long event and they would put down gag
lines, one-liners.

Jack delivered his address as if he were giving a technical
paper, complete with slides. He was nervous before this live performance but he carried it off like the pro he is, without a flaw.

Sitting in the audience in the big Biltmore ballroom, I
thought this was great. Here I had the head writers for both Johnny
Carson and Bob Hope, with "Mr. Carlin" the popularly unpopu-
lar character from the top-rated Newhart show delivering the
goods. It was all hilarious.

Jack would put up a picture of a Mexican Restaurant.
He'd say he asked Evan Campbell, the immediate past president

of the hygiene association who was from Los Alamos, New Mexico, "How can you tell a good Mexican restaurant from a bad one? Evan said, 'That's easy. When you go in the john there is a ring of salt around the toilet.'"

Then Jack would show a picture of another toilet, with a headline across the top that said "Microwave Toilet Danger." Jack told the group that he had been monitoring their discussions of the hazards of microwave radiation. He said, "I advise each and every one of you not - I repeat, not — to use this product because it will cook your ass in sixty seconds."

Some of the material was off-color but the audience - and I guess this shows that even serious scientists have a sense of humor - went ballistic with laughter.

He showed a shot of the BFGoodrich blimp. And said it had saddened him to learn that "your executive director, Bill McCormick, had been fired before taking his job with American Industrial Hygiene Association. When he was head of industrial hygiene for BFGoodrich he would take people to baseball and football games and proudly point to 'our blimp' riding high above Cleveland Stadium. Folks, I hate to tell you this now but Bill didn't know that the damned blimp was Goodyear's. Oh, what the hell, give him a break, both companies start with 'Good.'"

Jack went on for twenty minutes and the twenty minutes went by in a whiz, people were clamoring for more but he was through with his material. They gave him a genuine standing ovation and after the speech they patiently stood two abreast at least a hundred deep to get his autograph. Good guy, that Jack Riley, and one of Cleveland's own.

• • •

Speaking of whizzing by, one time Jack and Pat McCormick (no relation to the Bill mentioned previously) had worked up about a two and a half hour comedy routine for a theater-in-the-round performance in L.A. They sharpened and honed it so that it was just right. Performance time had arrived and they went about their business. Jack said they were kind of high-pitched and antsy when they got going and anxiety started lacing in, and they kept moving faster and faster with each joke. They got to the point where they were moving so fast they ran through all the material in about thirty minutes and there was nothing left for the second half of the show. "I believe we decided that night that theater-in-the-round was probably not for us," Jack reflected.

Few people know that Pat McCormick was a gifted high hurdler in his high school and college days. He raced for Harvard and came in first in the Millrose Games in those days when he was long and lanky.

Growing up in Rocky River and at Rocky River High, Pat was always a natural cut-up. In the 1950s he was working in Chicago in the advertising business when one day he met Jonathan Winters. Winters found McCormick to be weirdly funny and asked Pat to join him in New York City where he was doing a new TV show. Pat signed on and forever more was a comedy man, including his appearing in many of the sketches he wrote. Later, he even teamed with Don Rickles for their own comedy series.

But Pat's greatest fame came from his long work as the head comedy writer for Johnny Carson, both in New York and Los Angeles. Look at the old Carson "Tonight" shows on tape from the sixties and seventies and you'll see some of his best work, led by Pat McCormick. Pat, who by then had put on a good deal of weight and was a bear of a man, would come on the show as a New Year's baby, a turkey for Thanksgiving, a large leprechaun for St. Patty's Day and all sorts of other people and creatures, and the bits were hilarious. At one point, Pat, on a bet, crossed the line with Carson and "streaked" the comedian as he was giving his opening monologue. They parted shortly after.

Pat went on to a number of other TV and movie projects, not the least of which were the "Smokey and the Bandit" films with Burt Reynolds, Jackie Gleason and little Paul Williams playing the sidekick to the six-six Pat McCormick. He did a lot of the writing for these critically acclaimed comedies.

And he wrote and starred in a classic movie, "Under the Rainbow," about a troupe of touring circus performers all of whom were midgets. Seemingly, there were hundreds of them. The juxtaposition of the big guy McCormick as their tour manager was visually a side-splitter. These little tykes were nasty and cranky and were systematically tearing apart the hotel they were staying at, swinging from the chandeliers and dancing on the bar after McCormick suggested they have a drink to relax. Rent it, if you haven't seen this work. Wonderful fun.

I once asked McCormick who was the nicest midget he had ever met. He said, "Without question it's Billy Barty. He was so nice he willed his balls to a bee-bee factory."

Pat enjoyed working with Jackie Gleason because Gleason usually worked without rehearsing. "We'd bring in the script, and he'd just improvise; he was as good at serious acting as he was at comedy," Pat said. "It created a neurotic anxiety on the set, but the result, at least on Jackie's part, was always good stuff.

"And everything you ever heard about Gleason and eating and drinking is most true. We'd go into his trailer on the set and the greatest stuff would be lined up - buffet style. The best caviar, cheeses, fruit, an assortment of cold cuts, hard-boiled eggs, salads and desserts. And he'd have all the top shelf booze, wines, after dinner cordials. This guy knew how to live life to the fullest. We always ate and drank big when the 'Big Man' was in town and he always encouraged us to do so."

In the early 1990s, I arranged for Pat to entertain at the annual Marymount Hospital black tie fundraiser. He was greatly anticipated because of his many appearances with Johnny Carson and on a host of other TV shows and in the movies. Few people in the audience knew that Pat had been a track star in high school and college, a very successful competitor indeed, winning many medals and achieving stardom in Olympic-like world-class events such as the Millrose Games. It was my pleasure to introduce Pat to the audience and then he did his thing - wild-eyed and over-the-top comedy - the kind of stuff that made him famous. Everyone who knew Pat growing up or in show business or anywhere else knew they were dealing with a comedic genius, a congenial, nice man to be around and a scholar of the human as well as other species, so much so that he saw the nuances of humor that abounded in any situation where these species interacted.

Thus so, Pat was a favorite roaster at Friar's Club dinners in L.A. He did this so well he was a mainstay on Dean Martin's fabulously funny TV roast series available on tape. Some of this stuff goes back thirty-plus years but is timelessly funny.

On the occasion of his mother's death, Pat the Irishman thought the crowd at the funeral home was particularly maudlin and not acting in the true festive tradition of an Irish wake. He thought he'd better "jack up" the crowd, and he did so by dropping his drawers as he stood before the casket.

I once asked Pat how it was that he had acquired such a staunch sense of humor. He said it was all observational. He said growing up on Cleveland's West Side, surrounded by Irish people, gave him much to work with. He said his whole early childhood and teen years consisted of one practical joke after the other. Ah, the impish giant who should have been an elf.

Unfortunately, Pat suffered a debilitating stroke a few years ago, but those who visit him frequently - one of the most regular visitors being his old pal Jack Riley - say he hasn't lost an ounce of his humor.

One of those who keep in contact with Pat is Rocky River native Ann Elder, a multi-Emmy award winning comedy writer and producer who returned to live in the Cleveland area recently. Earlier, Ann was also an actress. She replaced Goldy Hawn as one of the zany girls on the top-rated "Laugh In" show and was in a number of other comedies as a guest performer.

"The Cleveland crowd out in Hollywood is as thick as molasses," Ann said recently. "We stick together and help each other when someone is in need.

"With the old Cleveland Browns we'd make a ritual of going to an L.A. bar where the Browns Backers Club held events for the games. You could go anywhere in L.A., several places in the Valley, a couple in Santa Monica, in Hollywood itself, and find a good time with your buds from Cleveland." Among the attendees in addition to Jack, Pat and Ann were Tim Conway, the writer Jack Hanrahan, and a host of Cleveland-born actors and actresses, mingling with the other Backers Club members, including accountants, insurance agents, lawyers, doctors and an assortment of other types who found themselves in Los Angeles but were all bonded by their roots.

CHAPTER FOURTEEN

More Funny People

Cleveland produces naturally funny people, and they're not all in show business. They're in all the professions and in the blue- collar trades. Just look around you and you'll find them, in your family, in the office and on the assembly line. Part of the reason for this is the ethnicity that abounds in Cleveland. Another part must be the water.

I don't care if you're W.A.S.P., Appalachian, Greek, Italiano, Swede, or Estonian, there's plenty to laugh at. Just like Jack Riley's character, Gates Mills, even W.A.S.P.s are funny. They may be funnier then the rest of the breeds, actually. If your family dates back to the Mayflower and it later moved to the Western Reserve of the New England Company, to Moses Cleaveland land, you could be very funny and not know it.

The origins of these people are probably English and the English are damned funny. Just look at Benny Hill, Marty Feldman or the whole cast of Monty Python.

What makes the W.A.S.P.s in Cleveland really funny, the ones from the East Side whose ancestors were on the Mayflower, is they don't know they're funny. They all tend to talk the same, out of the sides of their mouths, right or left, and it's as if they're giving a tip about a horse in the fifth race at Thistledown.

They belong to exclusive clubs, like The Tavern Club, The Rowfant Club, the Hunt Club or the Country Club. And they have a good time co-mingling. Put them on the West Side and they wouldn't have a clue as to routing or even where they were. To them, the West Side is a flat land, certainly not the foothills of the Appalachians that the East Side is. They would not feel comfortable anywhere on the West Side unless perhaps they were in Bay Village. Bay actually is more preppy than most of the places you'll find on the East Side. Ralph Lauren should open a store there; it could be one of the biggest sellers in the whole chain.

If you see a kid with mud on his face in Bay Village, that kid should be extracted to where he belongs: Collinwood or Murray Hill where kids naturally know how to get dirty. In Bay, everyone is clean as a whistle and essentially they all wear the same uniform. This is funny when you think about it. Where's the leader in this pack, the iconoclast that would break the mold? You could have a lot of fun by having a day at Cahoon Park where everyone has to dress as differently as possible. No guys on polo ponies as the insignia on your shirt or blouse. No penny loafers, no white dress tennis shoes. No plaid skirts, no golf blouses. No tennis bracelets. Parma attire is more like it. Another part of the competition would be: "Who can be the dirtiest person in Bay

Village?" This would be preceded by the world's biggest mudball fight. And then Bay Village could go back to being the pleasant, non-threatening community it is on Lake Erie and things would be right with the world again.

Undoubtedly, the East Side version of Bay, so far as dress and demeanor are concerned, is Pepper Pike, which is nestled in its own little world and wants to keep it that way. The one radical departure from this quietude that I can think of is the rising controversy of several years ago when the community was up in arms about the growing deer population there. The deer, which still are not carnivores, like to feed on the Pepper ferns, flowers and vines that abound on and around homes in the community. They also like to dart across the roads and smash up expensive Lexus, Jeep and Continental SUVs that promulgate even more than the deer do in Pepper.

Several years ago the city fathers decided it would be a good idea to engage bounty hunters, have them hide in trees on the property of The Country Club and The Pepper Pike Club, two private golf clubs that adjoin one another, and shoot the hell out of the rascals. This would be a safe way of getting the deer and not hurting any of the Pepper residents. But there are also many deer lovers in Pepper and surrounding communities and they didn't like the idea of Bambi getting knocked off just so some vine could live. It seemingly got to the point at which the deer abhorrers and the deer protectors were going to face off with their muskets on the same country club properties.

This is funny, but I'm sure there are people who will not think that it is funny that I'm making fun of their cherished and tranquil community. That's even funnier.

So I attacked regal communities on both sides of our Danube, the point being that even the uptight bring laughter in Cleveland.

I live in Lakewood. I'm weird because I grew up on the East Side and dared to cross the Cuyahoga and live on the West Side. I did this because my wife made me do it because she has a large family on the West Side, in Lakewood, Rocky River and Westlake. I think she even has some in Bay and Avon Lake. We have the whole scene covered.

I want the somewhat happy people of Pepper Pike to know they are not the only ones who are confronted with deer problems. At least several times a year we have deer running down the streets of the populous suburb of Lakewood. One even ran down one of the Cleveland area's busiest streets, Detroit Avenue, a few years ago, saw its visage in a store window, thought it was another deer that it could molest, crashed through that window and then trashed all over the store before having to be stun gunned to the floor. Last year I was driving to work on Lake Avenue, at the height of morning rush hour, and I noticed a large dark dog running loosely down the sidewalk. I thought, Oh my god, this dog is going to get killed. I thought it was a Grand Pyrenees, one of those beautiful critters that are bigger than a small horse. The closer I got, the more I began to realize 'twasn't a dog but a buck deer with antlers and all heading down Lake Avenue between the tree lawns and main lawns at about 45 miles an hour in a 25-mile-an-hour zone. I have no idea what happened to that deer because I turned down a side street so I wouldn't have to encounter it.

So maybe the deerstalkers in Pepper Pike have a point. Maybe we denizens of Lakewood should hire the same bounty hunters and hide them in trees at Lakewood Park and shoot the beejeebers out of any deer that approaches. We have too many squirrels in Lakewood, too. We can get them at the same time.

There is another way to handle this deer problem, without the carnage. We can herd all the deer from the East Side and all the deer from the West Side, get some mobile homes with vines on their backs, and send the whole kit and caboodle down I-77 to Bath, Ohio, where all the people like deer and where there is plenty of room for the pleasant, plant and tree eating animals to roam. And where there are plenty of plants and trees for them to eat. They'll feel at home because the people in Bath wear the same kind of preppy clothes that the people in Bay Village and Pepper Pike do. And many of the homes are similar.

. . .

For some reason the combinations of people and animals breed funniness.

When I was a kid, a teenager, my father Archie Watt had a friend Herb Green, who was a vendor to TRW, where Archie worked in purchasing. Herb was a good friend to my dad and he also was a fine polo player, playing for the Cleveland touring club. We would go to all the home games. I was amazed at the speed of the polo ponies and also the skill of the players. We sat near the sidelines at the big polo field in Chagrin Valley.

We were probably the only people from Euclid at these events, which seemed to be designed for royalty, the same way they were played in England and India where polo reigns supreme for the jolly set. Here in Cleveland people would park their cars along the sidelines and often sit on their hoods to watch the games.

The polo ball is larger than a baseball, about the size of a grapefruit and it is harder than hell. Almost every game my father and I would enjoy seeing one of the balls go through a windshield of an expensive sedan after one of the players had a miscue. This was very funny indeed until one Sunday a ball went through the windshield of my father's 1955 Buick Special. But everybody else just laughed and laughed. I tried to contain my own laughter and had to run and stand behind a tree so my father couldn't see my ultimate outburst.

Archie, half Swiss and half Scottish, was pretty funny most of the time, though he wasn't always trying to be. He proudly taught me Morse code and we would exchange messages down in the basement where he had his HAM radio equipment. My uncles were into this stuff as well. I could never understand why they preferred using the complicated code process when it was easier to use their microphones and headsets or speakers.

My dad's call letters were K8TUF. He worked hard studying for his HAM license and he was proud to have moved up from the Citizen's Band, the license for which was much easier to obtain and didn't require the extensive test that a HAM license required.

He was especially happy to get his mobile unit up and running. This was far more exciting than the Citizen's Band, because with his long whip antenna on the blue and white '55 Buick he could talk overseas from his car. Conversation, however, was somewhat difficult because when he made a "contact" overseas the contact didn't understand Archie and Archie didn't understand the fellow HAM in France or Germany. Usually the conversation consisted of "Hello" and "Goodbye," words that everyone understood.

He took me for a drive one Sunday to proudly show me how this all worked. I was about fourteen. We were heading east on Chardon Road, which was way high in the air, compared to our home near the banks of Lake Erie. My dad figured this would give him the best signal possible in the Cleveland area and from this location and eastward he could reach Europe. While he was demonstrating everything for me, he had to make a left jog to get around a slow-moving car on the two-lane road. He did this while holding the mike in his left hand and shifting it to his right and somehow in the process the long wire from the mobile radio got caught around the steering wheel and snapped in half as he twisted the wheel to get back in the right lane. I started to shudder and shake and then yuck out loud and was soon bent over gasping for breath from increasing laughter and pounding my fist on the dashboard. The more I laughed, the angrier my dad got. His demonstration had failed. His microphone cord was cut in two and he was now not only incommunicado with Europe but also with anyone in Cleveland. He swore a blue streak and then for some miles was silent, until he stopped at a traffic light and then he too started laughing and couldn't stop. And we laughed all the way home

. . .

If you really want to see some funny people I suggest you go down to the racetrack, especially Thistledown. These are people of all ages, races, both sexes, different income levels and they're all hooked on the ponies.

The A-bomb could strike Cleveland and these people would not hear it. They are focused on one thing and one thing only. Many are there by themselves; others are in small clusters with family members and friends. They've got the Racing Form in one hand and a beer or a cocktail in another. Many have ciga-rettes or, more artistically, cigars jutting from their lips.

Some of them do this every day, coming by bus and car. They're busy people, playing Thistledown and televised races from other tracks.

A guy who got me hooked on this sport of kings was one of the great Thistledown handicappers of all times. His name was Junior O'Malley and anyone who went to Thistledown knew Junior. He was a fast friend of former Plain Dealer sportswriter and long-time TV-8 sports figure Danny Coughlin. He was friend to hundreds of other disparate people as well.

When Junior's beloved wife of many years died, he was a mess. He was lost. She had traveled with him around the coun-try so that he could play the horses. Junior always said, "I would pick the cities that I would work in based on which of those cities had the best tracks, best horses and best jockeys. Junior worked for newspapers in the printing department and could always get a job in the old days.

When Dee Dee died, Junior was in a shambles with his banking account. She had always handled that. Barb McNulty, a branch manager for Superior Savings, took Junior under her wing and got him back on course, so much so that the 65-year-old be-came a permanent member of her and her sister Darlene's family. Barb and Darlene's friends became part of the Junior O'Malley Fan Club as well and would help drive him places like church and the grocery store and invite him over for dinner.

Junior was the prototypical Irishman. He loved to sing the tune, "Ace In The Hole," with the band at the Silver Quill, which is in the Carlyle in Lakewood. He always sang it well and with passion, his Irish tenor brogue unmistakably Junior.

Everybody loved Junior, who passed away nearing eighty in the early1990s. Each year, Danny Coughlin would have a birthday/funeral party for Junior because Junior thought he was going to die soon. Junior fooled everyone, including himself, when he lived a lot longer than anyone thought. In fact, toward what seemed like the imminent end when he had contracted bone cancer, he went into the Holy Family Home in Parma, where people who are destitute and dying go for their last few weeks of life. Junior outlasted a dozen roommates and was the certain delight of the home and its warm and caring aides. I visited him several times there; Barb, Darlene, Gayle Dregne and my wife Simona visited more often, taking him to lunch or dinner.   Danny made weekly visits.

If you went during the day, Junior would often be on the pay phone making bets. He always had the Racing Form, tucked in his wheelchair. And he was always ready with a cheerful thank you for paying a visit. You'd never know he was dying of cancer.

He lasted a good year at the home, when most patients go to the next world in just a few weeks.

Junior always enjoyed his annual birthday party and funeral celebration that Danny Coughlin threw him. Hundreds attended these events over the years and Junior always sang "Ace In The Hole" for them.   These parties went on for most of his seventies and there was no question that Junior truly had an ace in the hole.

His friends were special too, especially Danny, and Barb McNulty. Junior liked to say that even though he had the love of his life in Dee Dee, he now had the best looking girlfriends in Barb, her sister Darlene Fleming, Gayle Dregne and Simona Watt. He was right about that too.

Doug Dieken, the popular former Browns offensive tackle and now sportscaster and insurance executive, and Casey Coleman, another long-time radio and TV personality, were also close to Junior.

As was Cathy Coughlin Breninghouse, Danny's sister, and her late husband and writer/PR executive Bill Breninghouse.

Junior may not have ever had a lot of money in his pocket but he always had something better than that — a pile of good friends. Good Cleveland people of all walks of life who cared about him and who received much love in return.

CHAPTER
FIFTEEN

Even More Funny People

A lot of people in Cleveland know Bud Stanner, head of IMG Motorsports and a long-time senior officer of the company who has handled many pro athletes and developed countless corporate sponsorships in a variety of sports. He's well known around the country as well.

Those who know him will tell you Bud not only is fun and funny too but also one of the kindest gentlemen you could ever meet. Cleveland is lucky to have this guy who grew up in Chicago, then, after college in Florida, got himself into the sports marketing business with companies like Head Skis. In the late 1960s, he joined a young Mark McCormack and his fledgling sports management company that already had some big stars on its roster, the likes of which included Arnie Palmer, Gary Player and Jack Nicklaus. Today, of course, the company is a goliath group of sports and celebrity management, brand sponsorship and licensing, independent television production, big time events management (Wimbledon for example) and literary management, and I haven't named everything. And by the way, they have Tiger Woods. They have offices in dozens of countries, more than 3000 employees in all, with several hundred based at world headquarters on St. Clair and East Ninth in Downtown Cleveland.

Bud joined the firm when they had a handful of people and certainly was one of the guys who were instrumental in the great growth of IMG over the years.

I know Bud especially as a friend but also as a guy whom I've done some extensive business with over the years. Together, we were able to put together the Marconi Grand Prix, the CART, Indy-style car race at Burke Lakefront Airport that is seen on ABC and ESPN by 150 million people around the world each summer.

I also play a lot of golf with Bud and several other friends, usually on Saturdays and Sundays at Lakewood Country Club, one of the longest and certainly narrowest golf tracks in the Cleveland area. On many holes you are hitting out of "chutes" to get to the fairway and eventually when you get to those fairways, by way of dense trees on either side, you are then hitting to small greens.

Bud is a lot of fun to play golf with because you never know what is going to happen when he strokes the ball. He can spin it backwards, hit it off the toe onto an adjoining green scattering the people there, hit it straight up in the air (I mean straight up) and then actually catch it, pull it sharply to the left, completely miss it, or, yes, even hit it long down the fairway but not more than two feet off the ground, all the while chattering. I'd rather play with Bud than anyone because he makes you laugh and he knows how to laugh at himself.

Several years ago I was playing with Bud and two other pals, Bill Bartel, a lawyer, and Chuck Chaney, a sugar executive. You never know what's going to happen when we play.

On this particular Saturday, on hole number two, Bud did something magical. He hit a long drive to about 130 yards from the green on the par four 328-yarder. Then he craftily pulled out his eight iron and made a beautiful high shot to the green. It hit a few feet in front of the pin and fell in the hole for an eagle.

This was the single greatest moment I have ever witnessed in all my observation and participation in sports. Ironically, I scored an eagle on the same hole in the summer of 2000, but it didn't have the scintillating meaning that occurred when Bud completed his eagle.

Bill Bartel, who is a fine plaintiff litigation attorney who is especially strong in medical malpractice and is the managing partner of the long-time Cleveland firm of Miller, Stillman and Bartel, is noted for his garrulousness. Literally, within seconds of Bud's great act on the golf course, word had spread to all corners of the track. "Bud Stanner got an eagle on number two! Bud Stanner got an eagle on number two!" people kept passing on to one another. In some ways this was better than a hole in one and just as hard to nail down.

Bill, Chuck and I were happier for Bud than he was for himself, but he now possessed the golfing confidence that goes with having an eagle.

He teed it up on the 156-yard par three number three hole and smote the ball with a particular under spin that made it go backward from his tee about seven inches. He laughed, we all laughed.

This is what playing golf with a good guy is all about.

The particular foursome I mentioned plays the game by our own set of rules (I should add, only when we play amongst ourselves), which include as many as four to six mulligans (re-shooting after you've hit a shot that you don't like) per game. We have one at the first tee and another at the tenth tee and another couple of "floaters" or more on other tees. The number of mulligans to be taken is always negotiated just before the game starts. Some sterner members of the game who find themselves in this foursome when one of the regulars is not present consider this practice loathsome, as they do our "rolling" of the golf balls when we don't like our lies during the summer season when winter rules don't apply.

It's also fun to watch the other two players in the foursome play. Bill Bartel likes to take a big swing "over the top, past parallel," as they say. This maneuver can take the ball in three directions: one, very long and deeply to the right; two, very long and deeply to the center of the fairway; or three, very sharply to the left almost knocking the gonads off a service worker just a few yards from the tee. Bill prefers the middle of these descriptions.

Chuck is the best of the foursome, with about a 13 handicap. He never lifts his head when he is pitching or chipping and this almost always results in good shots to the pin. In other words, his eyes stay on the ball, an uncommon practice in golf that results in uncommonly good shots. But sometimes even this practice doesn't work, and Chuck can hit two identical shots off the toe of his wedge and be in the horns of a dilemma - the dilemma being should he try another shot with the same club for a third time and go even further to the right? No, he takes out his putter and snaps it at the top of the ball, sending it rapidly across the green, past the flag and into the back sand trap.

Bill and I have the same handicap, an 18; but we play vastly different games to get to the same handicap. When I feel bad and uncoordinated, I play better then when I feel good and coordinated. When I'm hitting it long and straight off the tee, I am toeing it with the short shots. When I have the exquisite, almost indescribable feel on the short shots, I'm in the woods every time from the tees.

Bill's back swing is beyond parallel and mine is short and nowhere near parallel, yet we end up with essentially the same score when the results are in. One thing is the same - we always have a good time, especially at the turn and after the game in the clubhouse.

What is also fun is that while Bud and I have similar careers in marketing and promotion, Bill and Chuck come from different walks of life. Bill enjoys suing people for the public good and does a very good job of it. Chuck is a broker and distributor of cane and beet sugar. For years, his family's company has delivered sugar products to big sugar users like Smucker's of Orville, Ohio. He does that well, too.

When we play golf we talk about sex, politics, sports, sex, the stock market, sex, history, airplanes and sex. We have a lot in common, as you can see.

Bill and Chuck have known each other since childhood on Cleveland's near West Side and they have been close friends ever since. Bill is from a large family and the first to graduate from college and law school. He and his wife Kathe are the two most giving people you could ever meet. Once, recently, when Bill won a big law case, he took both his large cast of brothers and sisters and their spouses for a long weekend in Las Vegas and then he later did the same thing for everyone in his office and their loved ones. You get the impression that he'd be a great boss to work for. Moreover, he's a great friend and so is Chuck, who is one of the funniest and nicest individuals you could know. No one is more happy-go-lucky. He relaxes you when you play golf, just as Bud relaxes you by entertaining you with his various exploits on the course and in the field of sports management. I'm pretty lucky.

CHAPTER
SIXTEEN

Good People, Doing Good Things

My friend Bill Bartel is not only a good lawyer, he also is a good person. That sounds like an oxymoron but not with Bill.

For over twenty years he has been on the board of little Grace Hospital in Tremont and has helped that community hospital survive, prosper and serve its unique neighborhood. He is now chairman of the board of Grace, which is now a part of the Cleveland Clinic organization and also has extended care satellites in other hospitals, including Huron Road, Lakewood and Amherst, and runs those very well. Eight or ten years ago no one would have bet that Grace would have survived, but survive it did under the leadership of CEO Bob Range and good board people such as Bill Bartel.

Bill has also been intrinsically involved in the big West Side golf tournament for handicapped boy scouts. Each year this tournament, held at Lakewood Country Club, raises tens of thousands of dollars for the cause.

And somehow Bill finds the time to co-chair as well the Lou Gehrig's Disease golf tournament at Lakewood C.C. and that one brings in at least $60,000 for the devastating disease that took the life of one of Bill's and my dear friend's son, Jimmy Given. Jimmy was the son of Dave and Carole Given and he was one of the star athletes of all time at Westlake High. Later he was an outstanding quarterback at Bucknel and had offers to turn pro with both the NFL and the Canadian Football League. But the disease suddenly hit him in his early twenties.

By then, Jimmy was married and soon to have a son and living in Boston, where he quickly developed a successful career in commercial real estate. But he died not much past the age of thirty, and amyotrophic lateral sclerosis had claimed another gifted and special athlete and man.

In honor of their son, Dave and Carole Given decided to start a golf tournament, modestly, to help raise some funds for research into the disease. That modest start has over nearly a decade turned into one of the Cleveland area's top benefit golf tournaments and now sells out annually for golf and the awards dinner afterward.

Bill Bartel and Bud Stanner have been part of the staunch leadership, with Dave, that has made this such a success. Dave and Carole have since moved to South Carolina and Dave serves more of an advisory role today, but Bill carries on the mantel for this important cause. Being part of the senior leadership of two major golf tournaments is a demanding task, but Bill does this with gusto despite an incredibly busy schedule running his law practice and taking care of his direct clients. But Bill, according to his long-time buddy Chuck Chaney, was always giving, even as a little kid. All I can say is we should all thank God for the Bill Bartels of the world.

. . .

Dennis Roche is the general manager and chief operating officer for the Greater Cleveland Growth Association. In his spare time he also does a good job chairing the Lakewood Hospital board of trustees.

Proving that people in the business world can be fun and funny, Dennis Roche is one of Cleveland's delightful assets. If he were a member of La Cosa Nostra, his name would be Denny "The Wallet" Roche, just like Jimmy "The Weasel," Joe "The Barber," Billy "The Guppy," and Hymie "The Putz." You see, Dennis has a penchant for buying and collecting wallets. This could be his avocation. Any time he sees a Coach or Gucci store he goes nuts. Even a Goodwill store. Anywhere where wallets can be purchased. And there is significance to his nickname if you think about what he does for a living.

On the serious sign of the ledger, our community is made better by Dennis Roche. Long involved in government and quasi-government institutions, Dennis is one guy who reaches above politics to get the job done, effectively. He has a rare combination of degrees from Cleveland State, one in English and another, a Master's, in accounting. Armed with both a verbal and C.P.A. arsenal, he is actually able to devour complex financial issues and make sense of them.

For a long time he was the Cuyahoga County finance director and held a similar post with the Regional Transit Authority. Three times he went on loan from RTA to help make happen three signature projects of the 1990s, projects that made the town better for sure. For one, he led the charge to establish the financing for the Gateway Corporation, which brought us Jacobs Field, the Gund Arena and many other consumer business enterprises in the Gateway neighborhood of downtown. What we had before Gateway was worse than bleak. Now this is a teeming and thriving area where people live, work and find entertainment 365 days a year.

Next, when the county got in serious financial jeopardy in the SAFE investment funds scandal, Dennis was asked to come in and get the mess straightened out. The guiding hand of Dennis Roche righted what could have meant a loss of tens of millions of taxpayer dollars in junk bonds and other bad investments. Eventually, through Dennis's efforts, the county got back on solid financial footing.

And a few years later, Dennis "The Wallet" came through again by seeding the financing package for the new Cleveland Browns Stadium. We all have fond memories of old Municipal Stadium and many of those memories are depicted in this book, but nonetheless it was a sports palace that some old-timers used to call "Soot Stadium" because it was so musty and dirty. Where it once stood as proudly as it could under the circumstances is a shimmering new field of dreams, a state-of-the-art facility for football and other events. It fits right in architecturally with the new Science Center next door and the Rock Hall, two doors down. Most people would agree that this is a better picture than the old stadium and a big, dusty parking lot that stood in this area before. Soon, it is expected, that the new Crawford Museum of Transportation and Industry will join these buildings in the same area of Downtown Cleveland's shoreline.

But it is significant that Dennis Roche had so much to do with making the new stadium a reality.

Today, Dennis, as general manager and chief operating officer for the Greater Cleveland Growth Association, works hand in glove with the former U.S. Congressman, Dennis Eckart, who is president and CEO of the organization. The "Wallet" or the "Roche Man," whichever appellation you prefer, also was responsible for righting financial difficulties at the Growth Association in the earlier of his six years there.

There is more to Dennis Roche than what I mentioned above, however. He maintains strong ties to connections in Tiperrary, the area of Southern Ireland from which his family hails and still has many relatives extant.

If you met Dennis Roche you might guess he would be of Italian descent, or maybe French because of the last name. No, he is fully Irish. His dark brown eyes, olive complexion and thick head of wavy salt and pepper hair might even lead one to believe his ancestry is Middle Eastern. His family is from the so-called Dark Irish region of Ireland, an area infused by Moorish/French/Spanish bloodlines hundreds of years ago. He certainly has no features of the blue-eyed, blond-haired, rosy-cheeked but fair-skinned ladies and men in Cleveland whose families hailed from the County Mayo region of Ireland.

Though he is from the "Black Irish" clan, Dennis is firstly and foremost a phial of all things Irish, carefully studying the land and its people and certainly possessing their lust for life and vigorous humor. And he likes Guiness stout, the dark draught beer that looks heavy but tastes light.

His dry sense of self-deprecating humor has often saved the day in tedious but pivotal situations on the Cleveland government and business scene and that is one reason people from both political parties have a good rapport with and respect for Dennis "The Wallet."

Cleveland is lucky to have Dennis Roche as one of its native sons.

.   .   .

Most people talk too much. But not Michael Glen Zimmerman, who is actually from Coshocton but has spent most of his adult life in Cleveland. He is my friend and close business associate.

He is often so relaxed that he can fall asleep anywhere at anytime. For example, when we're on the road together and having dinner at a fine restaurant, I try to take plenty of newspapers, magazines or a book to read, because I know he won't say much and is apt to just fall asleep. But nevertheless it is just nice to have someone there with me.

And one nice thing about going out to lunch with Zimby, as he is nicknamed, is if you don't feel like talking, you don't have to. This might actually be celestial communication or communication by osmosis. But it's good enough for me.

Mike is in his mid forties, stands about six feet tall, is light brown haired and bespectled. He is built like an Ohio

State linebacker, which he was. He was a "walk on" and "walk off" the same day back in the seventies but he has been an ardent Buckeye booster, nonetheless, since childhood. When he is not working in the public relations business he still busies himself by bench-pressing 400 pounds. He is also quite the acrobat.

One time, sitting at our beloved Theatrical Restaurant, across the street from our old offices, Zimby fell asleep for a second, did a back flip off his barstool and landed on his feet promptly alert.

He also is a deceptively agile athlete. Because of his over-sized biceps from his extensive workouts (this may be why he falls asleep so much), he plays golf in the most interesting manner. He lines up to the ball with a dramatically open stance, with his feet aiming to the left as if he were going to hit the ball deep into the trees lining the opposite fairway. This allows him, however, to swing through the ball with his big arms and usually hit it right down the center. He fears that if he struck the ball in a more conventional stance, he might rip his shirt or pants, which usually are too tight (to show off his body), and likely hack the ball deeply to the right, in sort of an abrupt ninety-degree angle.

Sometimes he is not quite as strong as he appears. Zimmerman, Dennis Roche and I were in an establishment in Key West and I asked our group if I could buy them each one of those "Slim Jim" sausages. I opened mine and ate it, Roche did the same, but 15 minutes later Zimby was still trying to open his. First he tried to open the shrink-wrapped package with his hands and then he tried to open either end with his teeth and couldn't do that either. Ultimately I asked the waitress for a knife and that finally worked twenty minutes later, to the roar of the crowd around us.

In spite of being built like a linebacker, Mike is lithe on his feet and a very good dancer. If he can't find a partner, he will often just dance by himself.

A Swiss-German, he is also fond of Wagnerian operas and will extensively sing passages from them to entertain friends.

Mike had an interesting birth. He was born in Charlotte, North Carolina, while his dad was playing for the pro minor league team there in the fifties. The team was one of the top farm clubs in the old Washington Senators (aka Minnesota Twins) farm system. His dad, Glen, was the first baseman. There was another guy you may have heard of playing third base. That guy's name is Harmon Killebrew, who later became one of the greatest sluggers in the history of major league baseball but first he became little Mike Zimmerman's godfather.

I checked out the above story with Killebrew himself one evening when I ran into him at the Theatrical. By this time he was a broadcaster with the Twins, who were visiting town. At first he seemed confused by what I was trying to corroborate but then after some serious head rubbing, he recalled everything and said that yes he had remembered Glen Zimmerman and his son little Mike, whom he indeed had godfathered. Small world.

That's all I can say about Zimby, except he's one of the good, solid young executives in town, a person you can always count on to follow through on anything, a guy with an intu-

itively strategic and analytical mind. But he's not totally im-
modest, because he asked me if I would put him in this book.
Now he's forever memorialized as he would wish and I can go
about my other duties without feelings of guilt or remorse
whatsoever.

CHAPTER
SEVENTEEN

Still the Best Sport

When I look backward, to today or forward, I still think baseball is the best sport there is to watch or participate in. The game has so many different paces you can be lulled to sleep and then suddenly there are two men on base, another guy hits a sharp liner to right and the first guy comes home. Then another guy comes to bat and hits a homerun. I also like the pitching tension of a one-run lead in the ninth inning and the Tribe brings in a closer. That's good tension.

Whatever the era — whether the game was played at League Park, Municipal Stadium or Jacobs Field — baseball always had appeal, even if the Indians weren't doing so well. You could watch great hitters, pitchers or fielders like Jimmie Foxx, the Babe, Lou Gehrig, Lefty Grove, "Big Train" Walter Johnson, Ted Williams, Whitey Ford, Mickey Mantle and all of our colorful players such as Tris Speaker, Bob Feller, Al Rosen, The Rock, Joey Belle, Manny, the Alomars and Omar Visquel.

Somehow, I don't get anywhere near the feeling with a game like soccer. I've never seen so much action where nothing really happens. I think it's usually true that the team that scores the first point in soccer turns out to be the winner.

I was watching cricket the other day on one of the ESPN sub-channels. There were no apparent umpires, and I couldn't quite tell what was going on but what was going was certainly endless.

To me, pro football today is too predictable. Every team seems to be the same, without any true signature to itself. Not so exciting running backs seem to run from team to team, as do offensive linemen and defensive players. Who's who? And whom do you identify with? There are no teams that have the color of the old Green Bay Packers, the Kansas City Chiefs, New York Giants, Chicago Bears, Los Angeles Rams of the fifties, sixties and seventies. Certainly, no one today can compare to the excitement of our Cleveland Browns of the forties or the fifties or even the Kardiac Kids of the late seventies. The last special, indelible signature team was the San Francisco Forty-Niners of the late eighties and early nineties. Now we have parity and things are pretty boring.

Pro basketball drives me crazy because you have to sit through a whole game of watching big guys going back and forth in front of you and it all comes down to the last two minutes. Maybe they should play two-minute games, play several the same day and get the whole season over in three weeks. Talk about ceaseless season length, there is nothing longer than pro basketball, with the exception of major league hockey, which starts in September and ends somewhere close to July. I don't know what's colorful about this. Precious nothing means anything in the early months of the season. Why go? And more people are getting the notion they don't want to, short of seeing Kobe Bryant, Shaquille O'Neal or Allen Iverson and a few others. For the most part, we are watching individuals, not teams. This whole thing is becoming nonsense.

But baseball I like and can take but it'd be nice if the season were 154 games again, so the World Series is not played with snowflakes falling.

Yes, I like baseball because of the many memories it delivers to me.

In 1960 when I was an attendant in the visiting team clubhouse at Municipal Stadium something occurred that would be forever registered in my mind. It was Ted Williams' last loop around the American League before he retired. Ted was now about 42 and striking out more than he'd like to (but let us not forget that on his last time up that season, and forever more, he hit a homerun). Striking out was the last thing this proud titan would want to do.

On this particular afternoon in Cleveland, the "Splendid Splinter" struck out twice. The last time, I could hear him coming up the tunnel from the dugout. He was hitting his bat against either wall trying to pop the encaged lights along the way. He nailed several of them. Then he reached the top of the stairs at the opening to the clubhouse and looked at me menacingly. I shook.

He did not take off his uniform top; no, he ripped it off, the buttons flying in every direction, and then he threw it to the floor and made it clear to me that he wanted ten fish sandwiches and he wanted them pronto. The head clubhouse man gave me some money and off I went to the nearest refreshment stand and got the fish sandwiches. And old Ted ate them without saying a word. One of a kind.

On the other end of the spectrum was a player who was up and down from the minors at will. He had been with the Tribe but later in the sixties he got a chance to play a little more regularly for the Red Sox. He could have been the thinnest fully grown man I had ever seen in a baseball uniform. He was so thin it appeared that if he swung the bat too hard he would have snapped in two. His nickname was "Goo Goo," a very strange name, indeed, for a baseball player. The full name was Garry Geiger. He played some centerfield and I recall that he was fast. I've often wondered what became of this obscure guy who returned whence he came.

The smallest guy in the majors at the time was little Albie Pearson. He was about five-four and he played centerfield for the then-called Los Angeles Angels. He was tiny but good enough to make the All-Star team.

The tallest guy I believe was Frank Howard, who was a center on the Ohio State basketball team before he entered pro baseball. He was a good six-seven or six-eight and really ripped the tar out of the ball when he was able to hit it. He played for the Dodgers and the Senators.

Another tall guy was Gene Conley of the Red Sox. He had also been a basketball player but was now a flame-throwing right hander for Boston.

The fastest pitcher in either league, by far, was Ryne Duren of the Yankees. He came to the majors late in his pro career, wore Coke-bottle glasses and often couldn't find the plate, which scared the hell out of most hitters. The only guy I ever saw in the late fifties who could hit Duren consistently was the marvelous Mickey Vernon, who could do pretty much everything well and could perfectly time Duren's fastball.

Duren, quite on purpose I'm sure, would always throw two or three balls to the backstop when he was warming up to further provoke the batters. They didn't have the sophisticated speed gauging equipment back then that they have today, but I am certain that Duren threw a good 98 to 100 miles an hour as a relief pitcher and for a couple of years he was instrumental in the Yankees' success at that time.

The two best-looking guys I remember from that era were both pitchers: Chuck Estrada of the Baltimore Orioles and Pedro Ramos of the Washington Senators/Minnesota Twins. Pedro later also pitched for the Tribe. Ramos was a cut-up who, with a more serious, less fun-loving, nature, would have been a top pitcher in the game. When he was with the Indians, he drove a yellow convertible and always had a lovely lady in it with him.

The other thing I like about baseball over the other professional sports is that it tends to breed characters. Perhaps there were more in the earlier days but I still think there are plenty today.

Hate him or love him, Albert Belle is a character. Deon Sanders is a character.

Even on today's Indians team we still have them. I think Jim Thome can be classified as a character, a nice character, with the "aw shucks" features. He looks like a big version of the kind of guys who used to play in Napoleon Lajoie's days.

Omar Visquel is a character, a naturally funny guy who also is one of the best shortstops ever. And, what's more, he is a hot dog.

The dearly departed Manny Ramirez also is clearly a character who plays the game as an idiot savant would. He is totally focused on hitting the ball and nothing else in baseball or in life. Remember the time in the 1999 playoffs when he was pictured like an "X" leaping high on the right field wall for the ball and missing it by approximately fifteen feet? That's Manny. And he is a totally funny albeit irritating guy running the bases, if he plays for your team. But he'll be, health permitting, the first player to knock in more than 200 runs, and he's heading directly to Cooperstown when he is eligible.

Back again to the early sixties and two other players stick out, Vic Power, and Leon "Daddy Wags" Wagner. Wagner may have set a record for speeding tickets on the Memorial Shoreway. Vic Power, one of the best fielding first basemen of all time and an exciting hitter, once jumped into the stands and was going to beat the crap out of Woody Hayes, yes, "the Woody Hayes," for calling Power a "hot dog" and "showboat" throughout one night game. Hayes was sitting a few rows behind the Indians dugout, and he and Power started shouting at each other between innings.

I don't think Power knew exactly what "hot dog" and "showboat" meant because he was from Puerto Rico and spoke only broken English. But somehow his pal Jimmy Piersall explained these derogatory expressions to him and got him madder than hell.

Woody, whose football teams at Ohio State decidedly were devoid of flashiness, didn't like the way Power fielded with one hand in a sweeping, scooping motion. And he didn't like the way Power batted, taking practice swings as if he were hitting a golf club. That was a way of taking practice swings that many of his fellow Kansas City Athletics adopted when Power played for that major league team. It was known as the "Kansas City" swing. Some people, and obviously one of them was Woody, thought this was also a showboat act to flamboyantly irritate the pitcher.

Well, I know one thing about Vic Power and that is that he was a most gifted athlete who could play any position but was especially effective at first base, where he was an All-Star, and during his time or most any other time, few could play the position as well as he could. And he was one of the better hitters of his day. He was also one of the few bright lights on the Indians' teams of that era.

In Cleveland, which is celebrating the 100th year of its entry in the American League in 2001, we have had three and four generations of fans - men and many women - who have passed down the lore of the Tribe in their families, and there should be much more of this to pass on in the generations to come and generally it should be good stuff about a game that will be essentially the same as it was in 1901.

CHAPTER EIGHTEEN

Why Cleveland is Cool

One reason is Les Roberts. The author of the acclaimed Milan Jacovich series of murder mysteries that take place in Cleveland, Les is a transplanted Clevelander and more committed to the city than most people. He came to Cleveland a decade ago to help set up the new Ohio Lottery television extravaganza and shortly thereafter moved here. He came from L.A., where he had lived for 25 years. Before that, he lived in New York and Miami, but, originally, he was from Chicago.

Les calls Cleveland "Chicago Lite." A lot like Chicago, just smaller. Midwest values and directness and you don't feel like you have to be careful of being hoodwinked like you could be in L.A.

To say the least, Les has had an interesting career. He was the first executive producer of the original "Hollywood Squares" television show and performed that function for many years. Needless to say, he has hundreds of Hollywood stories from that experience, from Duke Wayne to Wally Cox to Dick Shawn to Groucho Marx to Phyllis Diller to Joan Rivers to many more. He also wrote and produced a host of other shows. And when he was in New York and Miami, he was a comedy writer for the one and only, Jackie Gleason.

After all that, he prefers to live and write in Cleveland. Somewhere along the line he developed a penchant for novel writing and had already done a half dozen books with Los Angeles or Chicago as the scene set. Quickly discovering the nuances of Cleveland and realizing that not many people were writing novels based in our town, he thought why not do his writing here and develop a local protagonist, a Slovenian private investigator named Milan Jacovich. In the past decade he has written more than a dozen books in this series, which includes such favorites as *Pepper Pike*, *Collision Bend*, *Full Shaker*, *The Cleveland Local* and *A Shoot In Cleveland*. From his base here, he also writes novels that take place in other towns and have different protagonists. He has close to twenty books published and they all have been well received by critics as well as readers here and around the country. Some have received options from film producers. Certainly, the day will come when another Cleveland-based movie will be made from one of Les's books. He continues to crank out a couple of books a year for St. Martin's Press, one of the best mystery publishers, headquartered in New York.

Les Roberts is so well received by his peers and critics that he was elected to serve as the president of the Mystery Writers of America, representing several hundred authors, many of them well known such as Mary Higgins Clark, Elmore Leonard, John Grisholm, Dean Koontz, Tom Clancy and the late Robert Ludlum.

He makes it a practice to get all over Cleveland all of the time, for this is all grist for his books. He takes pride in the fact he can live a very decent life in Cleveland Heights in a nice home and do what he wants to do, write novels, for national consumption and beyond. I have picked up Les Roberts books as far away as London and Paris. He has a following, and he is inherently good for our town.

Les clearly gets it and he wants his readers to get it about Cleveland. He is just as comfortable in a Slovenian or Croatian bar on St. Clair as he is in the living room of Sam Miller, the Forest City chieftain. He teaches writing at area colleges, is one of the mainstay talents in The Plain Dealer's adult spelling bee that benefits the advancement of reading, follows the Tribe religiously and is a magnificent example of a dyed-in-the-wool Clevelander, and he isn't even from here. If you want to know more about the town, read his novels. You'll love his protagonist Milan Jacovich, who is a big, strapping former Kent State star football lineman now in his mid forties. He is tough but sensitive. He has a way with women, although he is somewhat shy, and he prefers Stroh's and a fried bologna sandwich to anything fancy. Milan Jacovich is also a sports junkie. There's quite a bit of Les Roberts in Milan. And it is clear that Milan loves his hometown, even though his cases can take him out of the country.

I had the good fortune of becoming good friends with Les a number of years ago now. We have a great time talking about Cleveland and why it has been good to us.

He has said, "When I discovered Cleveland, I discovered a whole new life that I thought I never would have. In L.A. and having spent so much time in the show business world, I was accustomed to an insincerity that just goes with the turf. I had a family and my kids grew up there, but I always thought there was something missing. Maybe it was my upbringing in Chicago, maybe it was the Midwest way of kindness and warmth, that made me long for something different. And I found that in Cleveland. I try to get my friends in the mystery writing business to come here as much as possible. I like to show it off."

And we should show off Les Roberts as much as we can, too.

• • •

One of the places where Les and I like to "hang" is the Velvet Tango Room, on Columbus, near Abbey on the near West Side. The proprietor, Paulius Nasvytis, fashioned this wonderful place with his own hands out of what was once a rough and tumble biker bar. Paulius, you might have guessed, is of Lithuanian descent, the son of an immigrant carpenter who came to Cleveland and eventually developed a successful home building and general construction company. His father passed many of his skills on to Paulius, who in turn reveres these gifts and the deep ethnic upbringing his parents gave him and all things that are his Lithuanian heritage, including his ability to speak the language fluently.

Paulius had worked as a waiter for a long time in fashionable restaurants such as "Johnny's On Fulton" but his real dream was to have his own place. I can tell you that it is unique, a throwback to the old elegance of the thirties and forties and even the fifties. An eclectic crowd gathers there and you can hear gypsy violin and accordion there and fine jazz. It's open from 4p.m. until the wee hours six nights a week. Waves of people come in during the evening, but there are pockets of time, especially during the week, when you can get your wits about you and have a quiet conversation.

What is cool about this place is that it is Paulius's dream fulfilled. People from out of town drool at this special Cleveland watering hole, and it is the place where Clevelanders like Les Roberts and I have our séances, and always a lot of laughs and information exchanged.

Another reason that the Velvet Tango Room is cool is Paulius's associates, Marybeth, the queen of Cleveland bartenders, and Linda and Randy. These are people who make you feel good after a long day's work. They are smart and kind and they are Clevelanders. Marybeth worked in Hawaii and Los Angeles for many years and found her way back home. She is bright and beautiful and knows the cardinal rule of never letting anything said at the bar get past the front door.

On the East Side, a favorite spot of Les Roberts', Milan Jacovich's and mine is the fabulously its own "Nighttown" on the top of Cedar Hill. Long owned by John Barr, this is a woody and dark English or Irish-like pub with good food and good jazz, including national acts such as Ahmad Jamal, McCoy Tyner and Ray Brown. Recently John's Irish understudy, Brendan Ring, who hails from the Old Sod and worked for quite a while in New York City before coming to Cleveland, bought the business and I'm quite sure he will keep it going as long as the thirty-plus years that John did.

Another place, one unfortunately that is no longer with us, was the long-time emporium known as Jim's Steak House, on the Cuyahoga River near the Eagle Avenue Bridge. That's where I met Les Roberts. He was there getting some research done for his books. At the time, he was thinking of moving Milan Jacovich's offices to the Flats, near Jim's, which is something he later did.

Great place for a steak or a good burger ground from top sirloin. Exceptional home fries and salads. Ray Rockey owned the place for decades and after he died things just weren't the same, though a great bartender, Ray Macaskee, continued to serve up some good banter and quips. The clientele was everyone from a truck mechanic to a big firm lawyer to a longshoreman to a public relations guy to a concrete executive. We'd always eat in the back and that's exactly where I first met Les Roberts. We made that one of our favorite gathering spots, and we truly miss it. The repartee in that part of the restaurant was among the best you could find anywhere in the country.

Back on the West Side at 89th and Detroit is yet another one-of-a-kind restaurant that is still going strong. Owned by the same family since the 1930s, Ferris Steak House is a place where you can get a great salad and a steak inexpensively. It has two dining rooms and on weekend evenings an old-timer entertains still on the piano. Not so long ago they had two piano players, one in each room. For lunch or dinner, you can't beat the food, drinks and service. The crowd runs the gamut, young, middle-aged and senior, and like old Jim's, it has an eclectic mix of professional and blue-collar patrons.

Third generation brother and sister Bruce and Mary Jane Ferris run the restaurant, along with a second establishment near the Gund Arena downtown. The one downtown caters more to the sporting set and during the summer they roll up the windows in the bar section and you get the feel of being outdoors. Along with their outstanding steak, lobster and chop entrees, they make a delicious tibuli and hummus dish and a delectable, homemade rice pudding.

During the winter, I like to head to the downtown Ferris Steak House to get away on Saturday afternoons to read, eat and think. If the one on Detroit were open during the day on Saturdays, I'd go there.

. . .

Another thing that's cool about Cleveland is that there are talented people who have left the city to pursue their careers but still hold the town in such high esteem that they tell stories about it - on film.

For six weeks in the spring of 2001, the Russo brothers, Anthony and Joe, directed a movie they had written, "Welcome To Collinwood," in Collinwood, Slavic Village and downtown and other all-Cleveland locales. The powers that be in Hollywood tried to get them to film the full-length feature in Toronto because it would be cheaper with the highly favorable exchange rate from the American to the Canadian dollar. But the brothers persevered, giving up part of their screenwriters' fees to convince the producers Cleveland was the only place to shoot this film.

This was the first feature film for the Russos, who had earlier scored an acclaimed film short at the Sundance Film Festival for budding writers and directors. They simply wanted "Welcome To Collinwood" shot here because it is a satirical piece about a group of penny-ante criminals in Cleveland who are trying to rob a pawnshop. Plus, they love the town.

So convincing were these young artists that they ultimately convinced Section Eight, the production company formed by Oscar-winning director Steven Soderbergh and actor George Clooney, to get the $10 million together to mount the film here. Clooney, who had a smallish role in the movie as a favor to the Russos, had a ball in Cleveland, standing on the bar at Little Bar & Grill, off West 6th Street, singing "American Pie" and taking in the hip Mercury lounge, nearby on successive nights after the day's shooting. Other familiar actors in the movie included William H. Macy (of "Fargo" fame), Michael Jeter, Patricia Clarkson and Sam Rockwell. The Russos expect the film to be released in 2002.

Of course, many other films have been shot in whole and in part here. The Cleveland area has a quaint combination of big city architecture, water, parks, homes, high-rises, small towns and rural areas that combine for some interesting landscape. I think you'll see more movie-making here in the future, from what industry sources indicate.

But the real cool thing about this is the Russo brothers' story and how they got Hollywood - big-time Hollywood - to believe in their first major project and insist that it be done in Cleveland. My guess is you'll be hearing a lot more from them as time goes on in the motion picture world.

. . .

Now I'm going to switch to another locale. Most people wouldn't think that a cemetery could be cool, but I know at least one in the area that is. That is Lake View Cemetery.

Nothing is more serene than to take a drive through Lake View or park the car and walk around. Funny thing about Lake View is that there are plenty more available plots there if you should like to "rest with the best." Not only is John D. Rockefeller and his wife buried there as well as some other family members, so too are a good many of the other titans that formed Cleveland during the industrial revolution. The Mathers, the Hannas, the Wintons, the Wades, the Whites, the Warners, the Swaseys, the Oglebays, the Van Sweringens, and the Brushes are just a few of the names from Cleveland's manufacturing, lake shipping, railroad, ore, coal and oil processing, and real estate development history that reside permanently at Lake View. Most everyone knows about the majestic Garfield monument that memorializes President James A. Garfield, but there are other monuments at Lake View that pay respects to many other top government leaders, including Ohio Governor Myron T. Herrick, U.S. Senator Marcus Hanna, U.S. Secretary of State John Hay, Cleveland Mayor and U.S. Secretary of War Newton D. Baker and twenty other Cleveland mayors.

Also buried in Lake View are Cleveland Indians star shortstop Ray Chapman, who is the only player to be fatally injured in the history of Major League Baseball. Charles W. Chesnutt, the first well-known black novelist is there too. So is Garrett A. Morgan, the African-American with many inventions to his credit, including the gas mask and the traffic light.

But that's not the half of it. Walk through the beautiful gardens and over the rolling hills of Lake View and you will learn a lot more about Cleveland history and the people who made it happen. Read the epitaphs. Enjoy the airiness of Lake View. And especially look at the graves of the not so famous. They and there families have stories to tell and some of those stories are short and simple, some are longer, but they're all part of what has made our town interestingly multi-cultural.

Lake View is more than 130 years of wonderful Cleveland heritage. That's why it's cool.

CHAPTER NINETEEN

A View From Fifty-Two

My office is on the 52nd floor of Cleveland's tallest building. From this perch I can see the whole damned town in all its aspects. A restaurant should be this high, so many others could have the view as well.

Some days when it is very cloudy, one might get the impression he or she is residing in an iceberg. No view at all, except for a surreal grayness that seems as thick as pudding. Another way to describe this sensation would be to liken it to an ant's view when he somehow got stuck inside a stick of cotton candy. The only reality of any color is the office itself. But looking outside, there is a vast nothingness from all angles.

Other days, the sky is blue up on 52 but down below rests a low-lying cloud that can totally obscure the buildings below.

On clear days, however, you can see seemingly forever and you can see quite well the stuff of what Cleveland is made of. On the immediate outskirts of downtown, in the Flats, down the Cuyahoga Valley, and at the mouth of the Cuyahoga River and adjacent lakefront you see a living Smithsonian Institution-like exhibition of bridges of every amazing sort, railroads, docks, mills, refineries, manufacturing plants, ocean and lake freighters, stone and cement processing facilities, the linear outline of the break wall and, lastly, a vast ocean-like body of water.

Looking south and east and also west you see buildings of various designs and sizes. To the immediate west, architecture from the Civil War and late 1800s eras dot the landscape. Where there are parking lots other buildings of this nature also once stood.

To the east, the Daniel Burnham-inspired malls and public buildings of the early-20th century are majestic and Washingtonian. Farther to the east are the more modern buildings of the 20th century but also plenty of others from the teens and twenties that helped set Cleveland's stage so well. The Huntington and Hanna buildings are grand examples. One from the 1880s, the Arcade (aka Hyatt-Regency) knows no peer in the United States. Designed by Smith & Eisenmann, it is often compared with the Galleria Vittorio Emanuele in Milan, Italy. Stephen Harkness, an original partner in Standard Oil, and Charles Brush formed the company that built the Arcade. Other major investors included John D. Rockefeller and Louis H. Severance.

When I was a kid I liked to go up to the observation deck of the Terminal Tower, then the tallest building in the world outside of New York City. Now, mysteriously, I'm looking down on the Terminal from my perch, which affords spectacular views of the finely sculpted masterpiece. The Cleveland Union Terminal, its official name, was designed in the mid-1920s by the Chicago firm of Graham Anderson, Probst & White, which also designed the adjoining Guildhall, Midland and Republic buildings, and the Huntington Building as well. When the Terminal opened in 1927, it was considered the state-of-the-art facility for passenger traffic. Today, it's still a kick, with the Tower City shopping mall occupying much of the space of the former passenger train concourses.

Then around the corner I can see first the Gund Arena, then Jacobs Field, two additions from the Gateway project that changed the course of Downtown Cleveland, packing in thousands of people to events in those buildings every day of the year and ratcheting up the economy for many surrounding restaurants, bars and other businesses for a long time to come.

Immediately to the north, the view contains the Rock & Roll Hall of Fame & Museum and, to its left, the Great Lakes Science Center and the new Cleveland Browns Stadium. Architecturally, these buildings are pleasantly compatible and are enhanced by the green spaces that surround them, including Voinovich Park where the old Euclid Beach Merry-Go-Round will find a new home.

On a clear day I can see a lot of other things too. Past Fairport Harbor to the east and past Lorain to the west. I can see into my old neighborhoods of Collinwood and Euclid, and I can see the majesty of University Circle and spot Cedar and Mayfield hills, the first foothills of the Appalachian Mountains.

On the west I can see the quaint areas of Ohio City and near West Side and out to Downtown Lakewood, and down the shoreline to the Gold Coast and past that to the area in which I live in Lakewood.

To the east, I see bunches of new houses in sub-divisions up lower Cedar, not far from downtown. Where grass grew into wild fields and rubbish flourished and things of all kinds were dumped onto ugly lots, people who once could not afford to own a home are now watering their lawns. I can't see that from the sky, but I can see it when I drive by. Looking down toward upper Euclid, Chester and Lexington I can see more homes, some of them big new homes.

You know what else I see? I see a lot of tufts of green all over the place. Thick, verdant greenery that you don't see in Los Angeles or Phoenix or Dallas or New Orleans. Cleveland was at a time referred to as the "Forest City" and from up here or in a plane I surely understand why.

Watching the ocean freighters and lake freighters coming into port is a whole other thing — especially watching the massive lake freighters negotiate the Cuyahoga. On a warm summer day the lake is also dotted with sailing and power pleasure craft. The scene changes constantly. To either side, east or west, I see the colorful flags and sails of these boats docked at the marinas.

From 52 on high, you get a great view of Burke Lakefront Airport and around each Fourth of July a primary seat for the Cleveland Grand Prix. And when the Blue Angels or the Thunderbirds are here for the Air Show on Labor Day weekend, the sights are spectacular. When the Navy or Air Force jets fly above Downtown Cleveland and whoosh by this high-rise I swear I can actually see the pilots' faces.

It is said that Cleveland, the city, continues to lose population, most of it to the suburbs. But there is something going on that most people don't recognize yet. Everywhere you look homes are being built or rehabbed, apartments and condos have been and are being converted from warehouses and manufacturing plants. Downtown, near downtown, on the outskirts of downtown. In the next several years more than 1000 additional new houses will be built on upper Cedar Avenue, many of them between East 105th Street and the immediate outskirts of downtown. Somewhat north, between East 55th and East 85th, a third generation of Slovene-American and Croat-American people are returning to live in the same neighborhoods in which their grandparents lived. And other nationalities are moving into these areas as well.

My simple guess is that the City of Cleveland will start registering population gains in the next five to ten years. My supposition is based on the fact that there is plenty of housing stock and plenty of places to build new housing stock, and you can do this at far less cost than in the suburbs. Fifteen-year tax abatement breaks abound and so do low-interest loans from banks.

· · ·

To me, whether I view Cleveland from high above the ground or on the ground, it looks pretty good. That is not to say we don't have our share of problems, the same any major urban center has, but this book is not meant to dwell on the problems. The problems have been dealt with many times over elsewhere and will continue to be dealt with I'm sure. No, this is a book about feeling good about our town and what it offers to everyone living in its environs.

Overall, this is a pretty good place to live. We've got more fresh water than most places. That will play a more significant role as the area moves on into its future. Because of that we are in much better shape than many other communities around the country, especially California and some of the other western states that desperately need water — water that begets energy, which they have in short supply.

Phillip Johnson, the noted international architect, who grew up in Cleveland, has said "there is no city in the world that has more freshwater shoreline than Cleveland's" and he looks at this as a great natural asset that we should take advantage of. Some might argue that Chicago has a longer shoreline. It doesn't and its shoreline isn't as linear, occupying dozens of miles on either side of the downtown area. Chicago simply has a better-utilized and more improved shoreline.

But let's not forget some of the improvements that we have made recently, improvements that are very evident downtown and will be more so with the new Crawford Museum of Transportation and Industry, and, let's hope, the planned Great Lakes Aquarium. And in addition to the projects on the shoreline, we can point to some interesting recent developments on the bluffs, just on the eastern edge of the downtown area. The projects include the new Channel 3 studios and the FBI Northern Ohio headquarters. We can build on these accomplishments and from them bolster our confidence to do more.

It also has been said that many young people, once out of college, go on to other cities to live and work. Of course, that's true. I have children to prove that point, but I also have one who was schooled in New York City and chose to come back here. He has many friends who also came back to Cleveland. My guess is far greater numbers of young people don't go anywhere. I wish the news media would interview them and see what they have to say. Many young people really like it here, and for good reason.

Everything is less expensive than New York or Chicago or San Francisco but we have many of the same amenities.

My observations indicate that many young adults have returned to our community after working in some of the other places for a few years. They come back, many of them, because their families are here and they too might want to start a family here. I think these people, the ones who come directly back to Cleveland from college or the ones who come back from jobs in other cities are in the majority over those who stay away. I also think the majority of kids who go to college here tend to stay here. And certainly people who go into the trades do. We tend to dwell too much on the ones who get away and stay away, and we also forget about the people who didn't grow up here but moved here and stayed here. I have many friends in this category who grew up in New York, New Jersey, Pennsylvania, West Virginia, Kentucky, Indiana, Texas or even California and other states.

Once people get here, they tend to stay, and that speaks for itself. That's been the experience that I have had with the people I know from other places.

CHAPTER TWENTY

Some Cases In Point

Terry Stewart arrived in Cleveland in 1998 with his wife Sally and her seven-year-old son. Terry grew up in "'Bama," as he is wont to say, which means the rural area just outside Mobile, Alabama. He has multiple degrees, in the arts, engineering, business and law, and by his own admission he was a professional student for 10 years up north and then got into a series of businesses in the northeast, the last of which was in Manhattan as president of Marvel Comics and their various other multi-media enterprises. Earlier he had been a top executive with a toy manufacturer and he was a banker, and, all in all, he had spent a good deal of time living and working in the New York area. His wife is from the New England area. And before they moved to Cleveland, they had a sumptuous home on a spit of land jutting out on Long Island Sound in Stamford, Connecticut.

In less than three years, they are dyed-in-the-wool Clevelanders.

Terry is the remarkable leader of the Rock & Roll Hall of Fame & Museum, a place he has re-invigorated since coming to Cleveland. And Terry and Sally have gotten themselves involved in a host of other activities and institutions in Cleveland, because they believe and want to make a difference, especially the Downtown Cleveland Partnership and the Cleveland Convention & Visitors Bureau.

But their greatest contribution is what they are doing for the Rock Hall and for music circles, including rock & roll, rhythm & blues and just the plain ol' blues in Cleveland and across the country. And they don't only speak the gospel. Terry's private collection of blues and rock memorabilia rivals any other collection - public or private - and is ensconced in his really big house in Bratenahl, on the lake. Some of his private collection is on loan to the Rock Hall and other museums. He could have the largest assemblage of Wurlitzer jukeboxes, from the thirties to the present, playing 78's, 45's and CDs, known to man. He has posters, original letters, Buddy Holly's homework, artists' contracts, song sheets, a wooden sign from the Apollo, autographed photos, more than 200,000 records and all sorts of artifacts dating from the beginning of the blues and through the forties and fifties into the early rock era, and what you have to say is the guy lives and breathes music.

As CEO of the Rock Hall & Museum, Terry says he has his dream job come true. "I cannot imagine an opportunity that does more to bring together my professional and personal interests," he said upon taking the job. "While I recognize there will be many challenges, I look forward to devoting all of my energy to ensuring the financial and artistic success of the Museum."

And he has been true to his words. Attendance at the Museum, which had initially spiked in the first year or two, fell to around the 500,000 mark annually but in the past year has begun to see gains. But more important, signature exhibitions have been realized, including a John Lennon exhibit produced by Yoko Ono, a riveting visual and musical exhibit on Jimmy Hendrix, and one about early Beatle Stuart Sutcliffe, his friendship with Lennon, his musical connection, and most significantly his art as a photographer and painter.

And beyond that, Terry has made the Rock Hall & Museum come alive with concerts from the early stars of Doo-Wop, rock, and rhythm and blues, and has encouraged local musical bands to perform on an ongoing basis. Most of these concerts are free and are drawing a wide audience. The best that can be said is that Museum has been enlivened with "live" performances appealing to persons of all ages.

Terry and Sally Stewart, moreover, have bought Cleveland, hook, line and sinker. Sally may be the best transplanted salesperson the city has. A striking, statuesque blonde with big blue eyes, she says, "We bring friends from different parts of the country here all the time, and we make sure they see the town the way we see it, in all its glory. They've all been impressed."

Terry, who likes to dress more like a rocker than a businessman but is an uncommonly good businessman nonetheless, says: "I'm more happy here today than when I got here and I was damned happy then. I'm not going anywhere. This is a good place for a boy from 'Bama by way of New York to be and I ain't going nowhere. I think I have the best job in the world and I live like a king."

• • •

I know two government officials from Canada who would agree with Terry. They both have lived all around the world.

One is the immediate past Ambassador from Canada to Chile, Lawrence Lederman, and the other is the Consul General out of the Detroit office, John Tenant, who serves a multi-state area in the Midwest. They both love Cleveland.

Both at different times had served as Consul General in the Cleveland office of the Canadian government trade development group. And both say they wouldn't mind living in Cleveland again, especially if they could have the home the Canadian government provided on the seventeenth fairway of Shaker Country Club.

Larry Lederman left Cleveland in the early 1990s to become the Chief of Protocol for the government in Ottawa, a job that saw him strategizing and organizing meetings with the heads of state from countries around the world and the Canadian Prime Minister and his Cabinet staff. Before coming to Cleveland, he had postings in Central America and throughout Europe. He feels like he's "home" when he comes back to Cleveland and is an inveterate Cleveland Indians fan as there is. When he was Ambassador to Chile, he customarily wore his Indian's baseball cap at golf outings and other sporting events. He was - and is - a Browns fan, too. He continues to visit Cleveland every chance he gets and the strong band of friends he mustered while he was here visit with him in Ottawa, Montreal and other places in Canada to renew the good old times.

John Tenant and his wife, Barbara, too, have lived in varied places in the world. They found Cleveland and the home on the seventeenth fairway of Shaker a place they have treasured. They visit here frequently in his position as Consul General from their base in Detroit. I'd say they know more about our town than some of the natives. You can even find the Tenants at the Odion, taking in the Canadian bands and other touring groups that play there.

I've had the pleasure of a long-time friendship with Larry Lederman and his family since they came to Cleveland in the late 1980s, and in the last couple of years I've come to know John Tenant and Barbara. We always have a grand time, and much of that is because of our mutual love for my hometown and their adopted hometown of Cleveland, Ohio.

The Stewarts, the Ledermans and the Tenants are sophisticated people who have seen most of the world and have met other people of every race and denomination in their travels, and, after all this, they rank Cleveland at the top of their list of places to live and destinations to come to.

This speaks volumes about our town.

CHAPTER
TWENTY-ONE

A Good Guy Named Sam

Cleveland will go where you take it. There are plenty of people making the town very good for themselves and their families, indeed. And they aren't necessarily the rich people. No, I'd say it is more the industrious, clever people who see a good thing and make the most of it.

I know a guy, Sam Smith is his name, who saw the light and made quite a life for himself and for his family here in Cleveland. Sam is a black man in his early sixties who technically was supposed to work in a coal mine in southwestern Pennsylvania, the same way his father and grandfather had done before him. He worked in the field for a while, a short while, and decided that he might find a better, safer way to earn his living.

His mother sent him to Cleveland when he was in his twenties to stay with relatives so that Sam could find himself. She must not have understood why he didn't want to work in the mines.

Soon Sam found work at the Ford Motor Company plant in Brook Park and stayed there for thirty strong and prosperous years, a number of which were spent in supervisory positions, especially in the area of plant safety. Sam knows every nook and cranny of the plant, from the roof down to the bowels. He knows every aspect of the plant's assembly lines and other manufacturing and production operations. And he knows the land and other facilities surrounding the plant like the back of his hand.

"If I saw something wrong, I'd shut that wrong down until we got it fixed and it was safe for the workers to continue," says Sam in his grande basso voice that thunders as he speaks. "The last thing in the world I wanted to do was hold up production, though, and I did it only when there was good reason to do it. You could say I was sort of in between management and the union, and I could understand both points of view. I got along with both sides and had just as many friends in management as I did among union leaders and workers. I think we all knew we had to get a job done. And, for the most part, we produced at an excellent level."

Thirty years in one plant with one company is kind of an oddity in these days of turbulence. Sam put his thirty years in and then hatched an idea that he had been carrying with him for years.

After working for a big company for such a long time, Sam wanted to become his own boss, have his own company. The area of endeavor that he chose was a limousine service. He started with one sedan, a sedan he always kept sleekly clean - inside and out. And he worked that service seven days a week, any time during the day and night.

He picked up a steady clientele on the East Side, then the West Side, making many airport runs, and also taking people to business engagements and parties or anywhere else they wanted to go. He charged them a fair price and always showed up - always early, when they were still packing their bags.

It wasn't long before Sam Smith had a few more cars and other drivers and he started to serve as his own dispatcher and business manager. The business became more and more successful.

Now, a half dozen years after "retiring" from Ford Motor Company, Sam has a whole livery of limos, sedans and vans. Owns them outright, too. His client list is long and loyal. He has two of his sons in the business and a number of other drivers. They all show up twenty minutes ahead of every pickup, and if they should not they had better have a good excuse or they won't be working for Sam Smith any longer.

Sam's dream has become a stellar reality. He knows the basic precepts of being a good businessman and following through on those precepts. He knows the quality of customer service is the key. This always leads to more business from other people. And, Sam still isn't afraid to take a fare himself, any time of day or night, any day of the week.

Sam fulfilled his dream in Cleveland. Sure, he could have done it somewhere else. But why? He knew the town; it had become his home away from his Pennsylvania mining field roots where you would live in a company-owned house, not much of one.   He has a nice house in Cleveland and so do his sons. They all work hard and for these efforts they can afford most anything they want.

"Cleveland was a big breath of fresh air when I came here - literally," says Sam, who is a thick-shouldered bear of a man.   He works out daily at the Jewish Community Center to ward off the stiffness of age and to help control problems he has with diabetes.

"I have such a good life here. I did at Ford Motor and now in my own business. I've got a good family, lots of friends, lots of clients who become my friends.

"What more could a man ask for?" asks Sam in his booming voice.

CHAPTER
TWENTY-TWO

Reflections of Your Own Lives

This book is written in large part from my own observations of the Cleveland I know and have known. These are observations that cover a span of time from the late 1940s to the first years of the 21st century. But this is only my story from my perspective, my prism. I know you certainly have yours.

I hope you do yourself a favor and think of the people who have made a difference to you, the people you have known here in Cleveland, people that have helped make this your home. Most of us have, or have had, these people in our lives. They are what really make the city.

Not long ago I was talking to a gentleman in New York City, a gentleman who is a star in the publishing world. I respect his acute intelligence and his innate ability to bring books to market. His track record is astral, but something he said when we first sat down to talk dismayed me. Not offended me, just dismayed me. He said in these very words, "I'm surprised anyone would admit that he was from Cleveland." I just laughed it off and sent a zinger back at him about New Yawk, which by the way I adore, in spite of the fact that it smells often like a sewer and its infrastructure is blowing up around you.

I've gotten this kind of hipster treatment on airplanes and elsewhere. You're sitting next to a guy from Philadelphia and he acts like Cleveland is a place that is the armpit of the nation. Hey, wait a minute, I didn't attack his town, and I could. When I'm on a plane with people like that, wherever there from, I just say, "You've got a good town there, and so do we."

Most towns are good towns: Omaha, St. Louis, Denver, Spokane, Hartford, Reading, Buffalo, Knoxville, Kansas City, Lexington, Toledo. Notice I didn't mention just the obvious larger cities, I mentioned some so-called lesser lights, but I've been to all of these and they are their own unique organisms. And they, like us, all have their warts too.

But if you have ever seen the incredibly large bust of Charlie Parker next to the Jazz Museum at 18th and Vine in Kansas City you start thinking what a soul that town has. Or if you go over to the Country Club Plaza area, the first shopping mall in America, which dates to the early 1920s, you'll see a thriving place that has stood the test of time.

Take a look at the new ballpark for the Toledo Mud Hens, which is right downtown in an area that was blighted for years. You'll begin to once again hear the heart beating in the city.

Take a look at the majestic row of manses just off the center of Downtown Buffalo and you'll get an idea of what Millionaire's Row looked like on Euclid Avenue before we tore most of the homes down to make room for other things.

Or have a gander at the white-fenced hills just outside the business district of Lexington where the horses roam.

Watch people go to the baseball games in Downtown St. Louis and you'll see a town of families. It must be a good town because many of its best professional athletes chose to stay there upon retiring. Stan Musial, Ozzie Smith, Mike Shannon, Dan Dierdorff, Jim Hart. Probably the nation's best sports broadcaster, Bob Costas, who is from New York City, has made his home there for years.

The personality of the town is its people. We have diverse kinds of people in Cleveland. Sometimes they don't get along, but sometimes the world doesn't get along either. We are just a microcosm of the world, and I like that we are.

Sam Fullwood III, the columnist for The Plain Dealer, wrote a piece about the differences between Minneapolis and Cleveland. He said, essentially, that Minneapolis had colder weather than we do, but it was considered a more hip place for younger people because it was more of a professional town than an industrial town. Now, make no mistake, Sam is very happy with his adopted town of Cleveland, but he was lamenting the "brain drain" of young adult professionals into places like Minneapolis and other cities because they find Cleveland too much at loggerheads with itself.

He quoted one woman who had returned to Cleveland after living in another part of the country. She was now 54 and she said, "The problem is not the city but its inhabitants. There's an edge to people here, a readiness to fight just about to the death, even when the last person left standing is in a heap of rubble."

I think we're talking most about Cleveland City Hall here, not the more than 100 city and town halls in the metro area. I like Sam and I like his columns but I don't think most of the government officials in this area are self-concerned wackos. Has anybody looked at the goings on of New York City Council, or Chicago, or Detroit, Los Angeles, or Miami. The same crazy political stuff that happens in Cleveland's City Hall happens in theirs. Central city management is not an easy deal anywhere today.

As far as professional jobs go, my guess is Cleveland has more of those than Minneapolis has. For example, we have the second or third largest law firm in the world based here, and many other large ones that prosper. The largest accounting firm in the world got its start here, Ernst & Ernst (now Ernst & Young), and still has a regional office here with hundreds of professionals. All the rest of the large accounting firms and management consulting firms have major regional offices here. Let us not forget that the largest celebrity management and independent television producing company, IMG, has its world headquarters here. One of the largest insurance companies, Progressive, is based here, employing a few thousand people. MBNA, the credit card people, has a huge regional center here, employing several thousand, and its CEO, Al Lerner, lives here. And we have two of the largest national banking and financial services companies here as well, National City and Key, and they employ a few people too.

And by the way, the Minneapolis-St. Paul metropolitan area stands for manufacturing and processing too, not just professional jobs. Ever hear of 3-M, Cargill, Toro, American Chemical, to name a few? The real name of 3-M is Minnesota Mining and Manufacturing. Toro manufactures lawn tractors and other lawn and home products. And Cargill is the world's largest privately held grain business. I could go on and on, but you get the idea.

I will say that the young adults in Downtown Minneapolis walk with a quick, peppy gait, even in the dead of winter, when temperatures go below zero. Some of this walking is done in a labyrinth of overhead covered passageways connecting the buildings, which is an effective idea in a town that gets mighty cold. But let me say if you ever go down to West Sixth and St. Clair at any time on a Thursday, Friday or Saturday night, you'll see plenty young people cavorting and moving quickly from club to club, just like they do in Minneapolis. The point is Minneapolis is not really that different from Cleveland, or vice versa, so far as action and opportunities for young adults are concerned.

One of Sam's readers had sent him an e-mail that stated that she fell in love with Minneapolis-St. Paul when she was there in college. She wrote, "Neither Minneapolis nor St. Paul experienced the massive white flight out of the cities that has so strongly shaped and segregated Cleveland." That is true, of course, but one thing she doesn't say is that the whole of Minneapolis-St. Paul had mostly white people living in it anyway. Where would they fly to? This is the land of Norwegian and Swedish stock and as far as I know they are mostly white. Don't ask an American Indian if he or she finds Minneapolis compelling. Most probably don't because they were never very welcome on their old stomping grounds.

. . .

My love stories are not about the bad stuff here or anywhere else. We have plenty of that to read about every day in the newspapers and watch on TV and listen to on radio. I prefer to relate the good things in a non-Pollyanna way through the people who make and have made this the truly and generally wonderful place it is.

Every town is different in its own stripe. It has its own lore and heritage and reason for even being. Most towns grew up to be big towns because they are on water, which provided the first means of mass transportation — and the first thing people needed when they were thirsty for time immemorial.

Even most towns that stayed small towns are on some sort of water tributary. Think little Yellow Springs, Ohio, home of one of my favorite schools, Antioch, a lumber mill, and a couple of restaurants.

We have our own Lake Erie, most of which hovers over Ohio and below our beloved Canada above. This is our lake and it is plentiful of H_2O, it has some good fish in it, it is largely no longer polluted and it should be around for many years to come. Other cities should be so lucky.

Hail to thine thy fresh water sea. Sea of great promise and great past, never to be taken for granted. Without you dear lady, we'd be in a whole lot of trouble.

CHAPTER
TWENTY-THREE

Why Not Fall in Love Again?

A *Love Story For Cleveland* is written out of pure and simple love for my town - and your town, our town. The inspiration for the piece came to me in the weirdest way. You never know how the muse will strike, but when it does it is best to take advantage of it and go with it.

I had just gotten my convertible washed at a hand-wash place on Carnegie, just below East 55th Street. The guys take a long time there but they always do a good job. It was a nice day, this day, and I thought it'd be a good thing to put the top down and enjoy the fine warmth of late spring. Trouble was I couldn't put the top down just yet because it was still very wet from the wash. I had an idea and that was to drive out East 55th toward the Memorial Shoreway, I-90 as we also call it, and travel east-ward. And that I did. I passed the Eddy Road Bridge and as I did this heading to Collinwood, just to get the roof dry, I swear to God, this idea hit me. I was looking at the railroad tracks on my right and thinking about nothing mostly and for some reason those tracks made me recall the great "Round House" out in Collinwood where all the tracks from the east, south and west converged. This was an awesome sight when I was a kid; it was the place they would turn cars, repair cars, re-arrange cars and engines and send them off to some distant place. I used to stand on an overpass nearby and watch this amazing, always-moving and always-changing scene.

Now the Collinwood yards were no longer there, I knew. Now there are acres of flatlands where all this action once took place. The action of commerce, as it were. As I thought about this, and I was getting off at East 140th Street, I began to enter the old neighborhood. A lot had changed but a lot was the same.

I drove, then, down to my old elementary school, Memorial, which is all boarded up but which once had been vibrant. It was where I had played "Father Christmas" (Santa Claus) in a French-speaking playlet about the yuletide season. My mother Molly had made me a beard out of stretches of cotton and she also made me a long red gown with white flocking and a long hat that matched.

It was also the place where, let me brag, I brought the house down one night when we had a talent show for the moms and dads. I was about eight years old and I played the "Julida Polka" on my accordion, at a time when that instrument was very popular. I played the tune on the big accordion my maternal grandparents from Slovenia had bought for me, and I know I did well because I got a standing ovation. I think I picked the right tune to rouse the crowd.

Now, passing by in my convertible, Memorial was dead. The place that had such beautiful flower gardens and a wonderful horticulture center was gone. The place where I could go into the music room and check out any instrument I wanted to learn to play had been long closed. The Cleveland School System had one of the best music programs in the nation in the fifties and Memorial was at the apogee of it all. It was the place where my special enrichment class enabled me to begin taking French in only the second grade. It was a good school of which I have many fine memories.

Then I drove past the Commodore Theater, a block and a half down 152nd. That was boarded up too, and the Memorial Library across the street now served some other function, the place where I was so enriched by the summer reading programs.

I drove on toward one of the gates of Euclid Beach, which was gone as well. Then I turned down East 156th Street, at Lakeshore and drove past Fanny's Restaurant, still a thriving landmark on the street, and I turned left on Trafalgar, and several doors down, on the right, was my grandparents' home, which still looks pretty much the same, except that there is no rose garden in front and no peach and apple trees and grape vines either. They were there when my grandparents lived there and I would recline on the glider swing on their front porch and read the books from Memorial Library. The colors and smells from their garden are still retained by my senses. Then I moved up Trafalgar past what used to be the pie factory on the left and I wanted to bring back the smell of the pies and fresh donuts, the donuts I'd bring back to my grandmother's house at lunchtime.

I kept driving until I came to the double at East 164th and Huntmere where I lived with my parents and I stopped there for a moment. Then I went on past the Grovewood Pool where I learned to swim. I continued down a side street off Grovewood and on to Nottingham and over to Lakeshore, where just down the street, I turned left on Lakeport Road. I had been on this street a few times before to visit a man I knew very well, a man who had just passed away the previous fall.

I drove over to Hank Geer's house on Lakeport, off Lakeshore Boulevard. His house, the one that is colored maroon on the top and yellow on the bottom. I thought of the man who had lived in that house, the musician and the man himself; I thought about what he had meant to me and how much I missed him and his pleasant outlook on life.

And then I put the convertible roof down, looked at the house once more, and breathed in the fresh, warm spring air near the lake in Cleveland, my town.

So that was the day I decided to write this book. I'm glad I did and I hope my stories, my romance about Cleveland, will make you think of yours. Just sit back and think, and the memories will come flowing and I'll bet it will make you understand yourself and your town a whole lot better.

About the Author

Ron Watt graduated from the "Happy Days" of Euclid High in 1961. He is a journalism alumnus of Bowling Green, class of 1965, and went about a career first in newspaper, radio and television reporting and later in public relations and advertising, including founding Watt, Roop & Co. in 1981. He was chairman and CEO of that company and now holds the same title at Watt/Fleishman-Hillard International Communications, which is part of the largest PR firm in the world.

His first novel, *Dateline: Ubi*, was published in September of 2001 by Greenleaf Book Group. He is working on three more novels, the second of which, *The Big Egg*, takes place in Key West. He divides his time among his favorite locations: Cleveland, Manhattan and Key West.

Send Us Your Love Story...

IF YOU HAVE YOUR OWN LOVE STORY FOR
CLEVELAND, SEND IT TO US AND WE'LL
CONSIDER IT FOR OUR NEXT EDITION.
YOU CAN SEND THEM TO :

AIRPORT BOOKS
660 ELMWOOD POINT
AURORA, OH 44202

OR

VISIT WWW.AIRPORTBOOKS.COM

Order Additional Copies
of This Book

IF YOU WOULD LIKE TO ORDER
ADDITIONAL COPIES OF
A LOVE STORY FOR CLEVELAND,
ORDER TOLL FREE:

(800) 932-5420.

OR

VISIT WWW.GREENLEAFBOOKGROUP.COM